Groupwork with Children and Adolescents

The *Social Work with Groups* series

Series Editors: Catherine P. Papell and Beulah Rothman

- *Co-Leadership in Social Work with Groups,* Catherine P. Papell and Beulah Rothman

- *Social Groupwork & Alcoholism,* Marjorie Altman and Ruth Crocker, Guest Editors

- *Groupwork with the Frail Elderly,* Shura Saul, Guest Editor

- *The Use of Group Services in Permanency Planning for Children,* Sylvia Morris, Guest Editor

- *Activities and Action in Groupwork,* Ruth Middleman, Guest Editor

- *Groupwork with Women/Groupwork with Men: An Overview of Gender Issues in Social Groupwork Practice,* Beth Glover Reed and Charles D. Garvin, Guest Editors

- *Ethnicity in Social Group Work Practice,* Larry Davis, Guest Editor

- *Time as a Factor in Groupwork,* Albert Alissi and Max Casper, Guest Editors

- *Groupwork with Children and Adolescents,* Ralph Kolodny and James Garland, Guest Editors

- *William Schwartz Memorial Issue* (title to be announced), Alex Gitterman and Lawrence Shulman, Guest Editors

Groupwork with Children and Adolescents

Ralph L. Kolodny and James A. Garland
Guest Editors

The Haworth Press
New York

Groupwork with Children and Adolescents has also been published as *Social Work with Groups,* Volume 7, Number 4, Winter 1984.

The Haworth Press, Inc., 28 East 22 Street, New York, NY 10010

Library of Congress Cataloging in Publication Data
Main entry under title:

Groupwork with children and adolescents.

Published also as v. 7, no. 4, winter 1984 of Social work with groups.
Includes bibliographies.
1. Social group work—Addresses, essays, lectures. 2. Social work with children—Addresses, essays, lectures. 3. Social work with youth—Addresses, essays, lectures. I. Kolodny, Ralph L., 1923- . II. Garland, James A. III. Title: Group work with children and adolescents.
HV45.G7345 1984   362.7'042   84-19131
ISBN 0-86656-338-5

Groupwork with Children and Adolescents

Social Work with Groups
Volume 7, Number 4

CONTENTS

BARUCH LEVINE, PhD, *Jane Addams College of Social Work, University of Illinois, and private practice, Chicago*

HENRY W. MAIER, PhD, *School of Social Work, University of Washington, Seattle*

RUTH R. MIDDLEMAN, EdD, *Raymond A. Kent School of Social Work, University of Louisville, Kentucky*

HELEN NORTHEN, PhD, *School of Social Work, University of Southern California, Los Angeles*

RUBY B. PERNELL, DSW, *School of Applied Social Sciences, Case Western Reserve University, Cleveland*

HELEN PHILLIPS, DSW, *School of Social Work, University of Pennsylvania, Philadelphia*

HERMAN RESNICK, PhD, *School of Social Work, University of Washington, Seattle*

SHELDON ROSE, PhD, *School of Social Work, University of Wisconsin, Madison*

JANICE H. SCHOPLER, MSW, *School of Social Work, University of North Carolina, Chapel Hill*

LAWRENCE SHULMAN, EdD, *School of Social Work, University of British Columbia, Vancouver, Canada*

MARY LOUISE SOMERS, DSW, *School of Social Service Administration, University of Chicago*

EMANUEL TROPP, MSSW, *School of Social Work, Virginia Commonwealth University, Richmond*

ROBERT VINTER, PhD, *School of Social Work, University of Michigan, Ann Arbor*

CELIA B. WEISMAN, DSW, *Wurzweiler School of Social Work, Yeshiva University, New York*

GERTRUDE WILSON, MA, *University of California, Berkeley*

EDITORIAL

Our special editors, James Garland and Ralph Kolodny, throughout their distinguished careers have been cognizant of the close relationship between the origins of the social group work method and early professional work with children and youth. In this special issue of *Social Work with Groups* their devotion to this linkage is continued and enlarged to include other practitioners and theorists who contribute further to an understanding of the critical interdependence of childhood and adolescent development with group and peer experiences.

Children in this issue are presented in the light of their total humanism. Only those professionals who have had a lifetime of studying and working with children in their natural play and peer groups can look so graphically "with an unfettered view [at] the painful nature of much of the social life of boys of grade school age." In these words, Kolodny realistically reminds us of a fact, well known to group workers, that in the development of the child the peer system can be either supportive or assaultive. He proposes that professionals working with children in groups have knowledge and skills for ameliorating the assaultiveness in group life and for preventing casualties. He suggests that we not by-pass this aspect of group life but rather describe and conceptualize how we deal with it. In the tradition of social work with groups it is recognized that many children may need help developmentally with their peer relations and exper-

1

iences and that individual therapy by itself may have only limited potential unless the contextual peer component in the child's life is also altered.

The two special editors in their own editorial which follows, share with readers their contemporary perspective while steadfastly maintaining their well earned roles as social group work theorists. First they have selected articles for this issue that search out new ideas for group work with children and adolescents from other disciplines and areas of scholarship (Hurley, Garland and West, Pfeifer and Weinstock-Savoy). Second they have chosen papers that present sensitive illustrations of practice which are theory based and validate time-honored principles and techniques (Malekoff, Wayne and Weeks).

The effort of our special editors to integrate emerging theory and models of group practice with social work tradition and theoretical heritage is an endeavor from which surely social work services for children and youth will benefit. James Garland and Ralph Kolodny, more than most, are qualified to give leadership to this generative professional effort.

CPP
BR

GUEST EDITORIAL

Group work practice with children and youth has exerted a strong influence on the value system, conceptual framework and technology of social work with groups. From its early emergence in settlement houses, community centers and child care institutions, through its street corner gang period and into its latter day proliferation in public schools, clinics and residential treatment programs, it has been both a creative pacesetter and a neglected step-child of the profession. Even as we write the preface to this collection of papers, we note the paradox. On our desk is a list, vastly expanded in the last five years, of new opportunities for student field education in group work with physically ill children and their parents, sexually abused teenagers and latency youngsters, and pre-school at-risk children in early intervention programs, to cite a few examples. On the other hand, we received just a few days ago an attractive brochure advertising a day long institute entitled, "Issues in the Treatment of Children." This program is sponsored by a large child guidance center, which incidentally has had for many years, as part of its array of services, a high quality group treatment program. What would catch the eye of the readers of *Social Work with Groups* is the fact that nowhere among the theoretical or practice offerings is there any mention of group work.

This omission is by no means an isolated event. We note the absence or cursory mention of group work with children and adolescents in many of the most popular books on group treatment in general and, sadly, see this trend illustrated in a couple of the most recently published group work texts authored by social workers. In the private practice field, group treatment of children is virtually non-existent. In community agency settings, child and adolescent group work programs tend to be poorly developed or erratic in their operation, being extremely vulnerable to the vagaries of physical space, bare-bones funding that does not include money for supplies,

3

transportation or food, case-biased intake procedures and poor group knowledge on the part of otherwise competent professional staff. Additional obstacles to effective practice are present in staff temerity and in a forbidding agency image. In the first instance, it is not uncommon for professional workers in all the clinical disciplines (excepting perhaps the various activity therapists) to experience considerable anxiety with respect not only to incompetence in the teaching of and/or participation in non-verbal activity, but as well with respect to the regressive threat posed by the activity and by doing it in the midst of "zooey" little kids or hyper-critical teenagers. Secondly, the agency image issues, having to do with the typical non-active and sequestered group format and with a popular perception of the setting as being designed for "sickies" or "little weird kids," means that most adolescents are resistant to being seen crossing the threshold.

Subtle status differences in the minds of professional workers may be readily discerned by the itinerant consultant when he/she inquires on an agency visit as to who is leading what kinds of groups. A distinction is made, with disturbing frequency, between "therapy groups" and "activity groups." This differentiation usually turns out to be made also between adult and child groups respectively. Incidentally, the "group-less" brochure to which we referred featured almost exclusively as presentors, psychiatrists; that in an agency staffed principally by social workers. Is there a double status message in this?

It appears to us that this adult/verbal bias exists as well in graduate curricula and among social work students. We note, for example, that there are few, if any, courses in group work activities (especially those oriented toward child, natural play activity as distinct from "exercises" for adults or for youngsters in educational contexts) currently being offered in schools of social work. This probably reflects not only a shift in emphasis on the part of faculty curriculum designers, but a lack of interest on the part of students as well.

Finally, it is our impression that the papers submitted to us for inclusion in this edition of the journal reflect to a degree the state of the art. First, the total number of submissions was surprisingly small, and some of those were rerouted by the senior editors of *Social Work with Groups,* having been originally proposed for other general editions. Second, some of the papers which we did not accept—and they were written by persons who are in other respects demonstrably skillful professionals—appeared to us, with all due respect, to be lacking in ways that characterize the present underdevelopment of the field. Some examples of this were: failure to identify clearly the implications of use of various interventive techniques in relation to personality structure of members; lack of awareness that there is an established history, methodology and rationale for "off-site" work with alienated adolescents, knowledge that might have better clarified what was happening in such a group; and conceptual haziness in defining the level and goal of a particular interventive approach.

The articles that were selected—and selection was based in part on critical reaction of professional audiences, although the editors accept responsibility for final judgements—represent some interesting blendings of old and new practice models and synthesis of various knowledge perspectives. One notes that the groups described made use of both activity and words in their operation and that there is reliance on the play and interactive rituals native to the everyday peer cultures of the various age groups. This is very much in keeping with the *social* traditions of supportive and growth oriented group work. Common to all the articles is specific attention to the psychic and social developmental characteristics of the age groupings as a guiding factor in choosing group models and interventive techniques. The concept of peer culture is implicitly or explicitly identified as a contextual principle and as a means of access to helping the children to make use of the group and to aid them in resolution of their individual problems and growth needs. Also of interest is the integration of object relations and interpersonal, peer culture theories, a development that is proving to be of great value in enriching the theory and practice of group work in both child and adult spheres.

We are pleased to present this collection for your critical appraisal and edification.

Ralph L. Kolodny
Professor
School of Social Work
Boston University

James A. Garland
Professor and Chair of Group Work Sequence
School of Social Work
Boston University

IN MEMORIAM

CLARA KAISER . . . 1896 to 1983

Clara Kaiser walked and worked with the great figures in our profession; yet she was modest about her contributions.

Her roots in the YWCA and youth service organizations marked her theoretical developments with a special ideological orientation so basic to our profession.

Those of us who were her students feel a deep and personal sense of loss. She was a teacher who exemplified individualization of her students through her caring connection with each one of them. In this sense she also illustrated what she had conceptualized about the groupwork method in her early papers, the simultaneous dual-focus on individual and group growth.

Her conviction was always accompanied by ebullience and a belief in the fundamental goodness of people and their collectivities.

The editors of this journal say farewell to a special friend and mentor. She contaged us both with her love of this profession and the richness of the groupwork process.

CPP/BR

Socializing Preadolescents into the Group Culture

Andrew Malekoff

ABSTRACT. This article focuses upon the pre-adolescent's experience upon entering a group in an outpatient psychiatric setting and it addresses the difficulty that the group worker often confronts in beginning the group. A framework is suggested within which the worker can effectively socialize the pre-adolescent into the group culture.

The world is full of the sound of waves
The little fishes abandoning themselves to the waves
dance and sing and play, but who knows the
heart of the sea, a hundred feet down?
Who knows its depth?—Eiji Yoshikawa, *Musashi*[20,p. 970]

Introduction

The process of socializing the pre-adolescent into the "group work" culture can be a challenging and exciting experience for the group worker, however, it is quite often a baffling and frustrating ordeal. The nine to fourteen year old, who is somewhere between the fifth and eighth grades, balks at play therapy, suspicious of the ulterior motive, which goes unquestioned by the younger child. Their suspicion about play is equaled only by their distaste for talk, especially insight oriented talk. If play and talk are taboo then the

Andrew Malekoff, ACSW is with North Shore Child Guidance Center, Manhasset, New York, 11030.
This paper was originally submitted for presentation at the Fourth Annual Symposium on the Advancement of Social Work with Groups, Toronto, Canada, October 21-23, 1982.

7

group worker is often left with clusters of insipid behavior ranging from prolonged conspired silences to unprovoked contagious giggling, to symphonies of cacophonous noisemaking. What is a group worker to do?

The purpose of this paper is to sensitize the reader to the experience of the pre-adolescent upon referral to a therapy group and to familiarize the group worker with methods of acculturating the members into the group life. The examples given are drawn from practice in the North Shore Child Guidance Center.* In order to achieve the stated purpose five themes will be explored using clinical vignettes to illustrate. These five are: (1) discovering the group purpose, (2) searching for the common ground, (3) awareness of the normative crisis, (4) the promotion of playfulness in the service of chumship and (5) the establishment of group rituals.

Flashes

It's much easier to ride the horse
in the direction he's going.[3]

Fritz Redl asks rhetorically of the pre-adolescent, "fish, fowl or human?[13, p. 2] With this in mind one need not question Baruch Levine's assertion that the therapist working with pre-adolescent groups may experience a "recurrent feeling of futility."[11, p. 23] It is in this spirit that the group worker must realize that group meetings with pre-adolescents will not proceed in accordance with *Robert's Rules of Order.* The experience is more akin to being exiled on to the canvas of an abstract painting during its creation. Therefore, the aforementioned five point mosaic would be incomplete without acknowledging the constant static, the unchanneled energy which pervades the group session.

A combination of the extreme use of denial and the seemingly chaotic process of (pre-adolescent) groups lead many adult therapists to despair that nothing meaningful is or can be ac-

---

*North Shore Child Guidance Center is licensed and supported by the New York State Office of Mental Health and Nassau County Department of Mental Health. It is supported by United Way of Long Island, United Community Fund of Great Neck, United Fund of Manhasset, United Community Chest of Port Washington. The Center is a member of the American Association of Psychiatric Services for children and the Psychiatric Outpatient Centers of America.

complished. (Group workers) have left many (pre-adolescent) therapy group meetings feeling that they could have been doing something more productive with their time.[11, p. 23]

The worker must gauge himself in order to find the necessary balance between tolerance and over control. He must also move quickly so as not to miss what's flashing by, for it is these flashes which provide the spark to ignite the group.

That which is unique and worthwhile
in us makes itself felt
only in flashes
If we do not know how to catch
and savor these flashes,
we are without growth and
without exhilaration.[17, p. 88]

Static

Following an evaluation, disposition, recommendation for group therapy and preliminary meeting with each group member and his parents, the group begins. (The preceding is simply stated, however, more complicated to achieve effectively. Groups may be thwarted from the beginning because of mishandling of this preliminary process, which will not be detailed here.) When the group meets for the first time there is much confusion around what we are all up to. Typical opening remarks, despite careful preparation include: "why are we here," "when is this class over," "I told my mother that this is the last time that I'm coming," "is this room bugged," "I can't come anymore because my favorite television show is on at this time," etc. The non-verbal behavior may include the following: restrained restlessness (don't fret, unrestrained restlessness comes a little later on), darting eyes (searching for bugging devices or the titles of the "shrink's" books), front legs of all chairs elevated about one foot off the floor and back rests planted firmly on the wall (the wall soon reveals an indelible signature of back rest compressions) and the subtle scavenger hunt for an object to hold on to, are but a few. When the verbal and non-verbal behavior are integrated one observes caution, apprehension, curiosity, suspicion and restrained energy. All of this occurs instantaneously, yet perpetually. A glance at the clock reveals that only a minute has passed.

Discovering the Group Purpose

The "why are we here" and "where arc we headed," or the purpose of the group can be most easily discovered if the worker respects the members' past group experiences and begins to educate through them. The following example is drawn from a group of five boys who were just beginning a group in the Child Guidance Center. All five boys presented socialization problems, low self esteem and at least mild depression. They were all twelve to thirteen years old.

Worker: Have any of you ever been in a group before?
Unanimously: No (most likely inferring *this* kind of group).
Worker: No, I mean any kind of group, not like here, like Little League, Scouts, a club or something like that.
Sam: I'm in Little League.
Peter: I'm in the Squires.
Chris: What's that?
Peter: My father is in the Knights of Columbus and the kids meet once a week.

Of course there are those who cannot think of any group that they've been a part of. It then becomes the worker's task to help them to find one, even if it is as highly structured as the school class. Eventually every member has a frame of reference, a group that they have belonged to.

Worker: Well, every group gets together for some reason, for some purpose. Sam, what do you think is the purpose of Little League, why do you play?
Sam: I don't know.
Worker: Well why did you join?
Sam: To play.
Worker: What do you other guys think might be the purpose of playing Little League? What do you think Sam gets out of it?

Eventually what can be drawn out are several purposes including: for fun, to learn skills, to listen to the coach, to meet new kids, to cooperate with others, and so on. At some point the worker can summarize by saying something like this: "So the purpose of the Little League group, I mean team, is to learn skills, to learn to follow directions, to work together with others and to have fun.'' This way of approaching purpose can be applied to Girl Scouts, camp groups, clubs, etc. After this process has been exhausted the next step is to begin to develop a sense that *this too* is a group and *this too* has a purpose. The reader might find the above to be simplistic and it is, however the implications are profound. Out of purpose one derives the opportunity for belonging, the experience of mutuality and the potential for change. Using the societal frames of reference indicated in the simple style suggested the group members are enabled to affiliate in a more informed and well grounded manner.

> A dozen strangers may be lying around, unrelated however, if a drowning person is spotted they become a group in that they now have a purpose.[19]

The group purpose is not static, it becomes more sophisticated over time. The initial purpose of the above group was simply "to make friends," and then "to learn how to cope with teasing," and later "to recognize when we provoke others" and at a still later point "to better understand our sad feelings." In another group of nine year old boys with poor impulse control, an early purpose was "to learn to behave better." As the group developed it became: "to learn to think before acting." The worker must recognize the dynamic, evolving nature of purpose and that the leitmotif of every purpose is mutuality.

Harry Stack Sullivan has made an important distinction between cooperation and collaboration, two differential phases of mutuality. The latter, he has said develops as the pre-adolescent "need for interpersonal intimacy"[16, p. 246] becomes manifest.

> In pre-adolescence not only do people occupy themselves in moving toward a common, more-or-less impersonal objective, such as the success of "our team" or the discomfiture of "our teacher," as they might have done in the juvenile era, but they also, specifically and increasingly (move beyond). . .the give and take of the juvenile era and towards collaboration. . .a great step forward from cooperation—*I* play according to the rules of the game, to preserve *my* prestige and feeling of superiority and merit. When we collaborate, it is a matter of *we*.[16, p. 246]

Searching for the Common Ground[14]

If the group purpose is "what brings us together and what directs us" then the common ground is "that which connects us." Whenever we meet a stranger on a train, if we happen to strike up a conversation, and if it lasts we eventually settle down on a common ground whether it be politics, sports, fashion or the poor service provided by the train and our current, accompanying discomfort. The common ground can be sought on different levels and it is the job of the worker to lead the search and to make the elements "which connect us" *overt.* The following four examples will serve to illustrate:

1. *Mutual feelings upon entering the group.* In the boys' group the early meetings involved a search for "bugs" or tape recorders and questions about whether or not the walls were thin enough to be heard through. Ultimately this led to the crisis of establishing trust in the group. As necessary as is the establishment of trust and confidentiality it is secondary to the careful process of getting there. Getting there for this group included apprehension in the here and now, fear that the intrusiveness of particular parents may preclude confidentiality and certainty that the worker (like a teacher) will supply a periodic "report card."

2. *The sharing of outside interests.* In another group of ten year old boys one of them, Carl, states that he cannot return for any more meetings because he's missing his favorite show, the "Little Rascals." The others recognize the popular show and the worker begins to encourage the sharing of their favorite characters and episodes. Although the boys are awkward at this juncture, the worker's fortunate knowledge of the "Little Rascals" allows him to model this kind of sharing. If the worker, intent on getting to the "deep stuff," views the discussion of a television show (or other seemingly trivial matter) as superficial, as a sign of resistance or as counterproductive, then he misses the opportunity to reach for the more profound aspects of the experience. The sharing of outside interests, the experience of actually being listened to and the enjoyment of being a *part* of a discussion need to be carefully cultivated. The "Little Rascals" example has symbolic meaning in that it represents a group of mischievous, fun loving kids. More important, however, was the sad possibility that this live experience would never equal the vicarious pleasure derived from watching the show (but there was also the hope that it might). As this group progressed beyond a

year together, Carl began to playfully assign nicknames to the others and to himself (Spanky, Alfalfa, Buckwheat).

3. *The emergence of interpersonal styles.* Just prior to the first meeting of a "duo therapy group"[6] with two ten year old girls, they sat in the waiting room not having been previously introduced. Carol was wearing a Girl Scout uniform and Nicole was busy attending to the "ace bandage" which was conspicuously wrapped around her right ankle. As the worker greeted them he asked them to follow him up the stairs. The "Girl Scout" spontaneously went to the assistance of her soon to be partner who managed to dramatize her "disability" just enough. The moment on the stairs illustrated, interactionally, what was to become a major focus of therapy: the complimentary nature of the compulsive, dutiful helper and the histrionic, impulsive victim. The common ground had been established, the challenge then became to make it overt. This was accomplished by suggesting that we make two lists: one of rules and the other of activities in the group. Guess who wanted to write the rules? Guess who couldn't think of any? As we proceeded it became Carol's "job" to help Nicole to be less impulsive, less dramatic and more down to earth, and it became Nicole's job to help Carol to be less compulsive and more flexible.

4. *The group name.* The following is drawn from the first group experience of a psychology intern.* Three girls: Diane, Barb and Toni (9, 10 and 11), were brought together for group therapy mainly because of their difficulties centered around poor socialization skills. Toni displayed a tendency to withdraw from others and was found frequently to lie and steal. Diane had poor impulse control, was prone to bouts of uncontrollable behavior and was quite self centered. Barb was noted to have difficulty getting along with peers and adults because of extreme "bossiness," excessive demands and the desire to always "get her way."

In the very first session the girls were observably anxious and expressed anger at being brought together in this type of setting. Barb stated her position firmly at the outset, "I'm not crazy, I don't have to be here!" In addition to promoting some discussion of the girls' fears and clarifying some basic procedures, one of the techniques used by the worker to enhance formation of the group, was to suggest that the girls decide on a name for themselves. The girls became interested in this and were able to shift their focus from

---

*Thanks to Ronda Fein.

reasons why they *shouldn't* be together to discovering some commonalities amongst themselves. One suggested that they be called the "crazy mixed up kids." The girls giggled about this and suddenly, the notion that they had problems was no longer a grounds for conflict but a place from which they could begin to work together. One of the others, however, suggested that they think of other ideas and the rest agreed. As they came up with names like, "the flowers" and "the stars," they were able to find out about each other, their likes and dislikes. Finally, one suggested "the kittens" and the girls discovered that they all had a love for animals and that each of them owned a cat. Thus, they unanimously agreed that they be called "the kittens."

The four examples are but a sample of possible inroads towards discovering the common ground. Absent from the discussion thus far are stressful life situations such as parental separation, death, alcoholism in the family, placement in a "special class" in school, etc. Geographical, ethnic and other familial themes may also constitute a common ground. The possibilities are endless.

Awareness of the Normative Crisis

In the style of the four questions asked during the Jewish Passover Seder, the new group member asks herself, "how is this group different from all other groups?" The exodus, in this case is from a more traditional system of values, to the experience of normative shock and finally to a new set of values for a new culture. The rules and regimen of the classroom, family, club, etc., evaporate as the new group unfolds. This is compounded when

> the worker gives tacit acceptance to the expression of anti social feelings (and) the familiar restraints are broken down. At the same time, the protection and expiatory comfort afforded by punishment are absent. The two conditions together make for an anxiety filled emotional vacuum.[7, p. 44]

The following is an example of the kind of internal dialogue that might be experienced by the pre-adolescent upon beginning a new group experience.

> This place is weird, it's the joint, the nut house. . .what the hell is going on here?. . .What am *I* doing here?. . .I raise my

hand to speak and the teacher tells me I don't have to raise my hand to speak here. . .I ask how long the class is going to meet and he tells me that it isn't a class. . .that crazy looking kid in the corner curses and gives the faggy looking kid the finger and tells him he'll kick his ass if he doesn't quit smiling. . .one of the kids called the teacher by his first name. . .what the hell is going on here?

The group worker's awareness at this juncture, his empathy, allows him to gently move the group into new and ultimately more intimate territory. This previously unexplored territory will constitute the groundwork for a higher level of interpersonal relatedness, an interest in someone of the same sex who becomes a close friend.

The manifestation of the need for interpersonal intimacy marks the developmental epoch of pre-adolescence. Nothing remotely like it has ever appeared before. All of you who have children are sure that your children love you; when you say that, you are expressing a pleasant illusion. But if you will look very closely at one of your children when he finally finds a chum somewhere between eight and a half and ten—you will discover something very different in the relationship—namely, that your child begins to develop a real sensitivity to what matters to another person. And this is not in the sense of "what should I do to get what I want," but "what should I do to contribute to the happiness or to support the prestige and feeling of worth-whileness of my chum."[16, p. 245]

The Promotion of Playfulness

the reason you got scared and quit is because you felt too damn important. . .feeling important makes one feel heavy, clumsy and vain. To be a man of knowledge one needs to be light and fluid.—Don Juan to Carlos Castenada, *A Separate Reality*[2, pp. 7,8]

Early on reference was made to the pre-adolescent's reluctance to use play materials or to talk insightfully in the group. For the worker the integrative solution is to make use of "playful talk." Playful talk is the language of the brain's right hemisphere which specializes in the "holistic grasping of complex relationships, patterns, configurations and structures."[18, p. 22] The timely use of playful talk can serve to mobilize the group during chaotic moments and to energize the group during more stagnant periods. One example of this kind of language is the "play on words." A particularly withdrawn thirteen year old member of a boys' group turned to the worker in the middle of a discussion which obviously bored him and he whispered "I wanna leave now, please." The group was momentarily silenced and Doug was asked to present his request to the group which he reluctantly did, "I wanna leave." The worker pointed to the plant on his desk and replied, "you can't have a 'leave,' for if you take one away the others will miss it." This led to at least a moment of more confusion, then laughter and finally a spontaneous group decision to make the plant a group member. It was then decided to name the plant. The boy who first requested leave named the plant "Lief Green," and instead of losing a member one was gained.

A crucial factor in the development of relatedness to another is the creation of the playful feeling. This is to be differentiated from the simple activity of play which does not necessarily require a feeling of relatedness.

> Whatever direct discussions of significant problems, issues and feelings take place are all to the good, but they are not essential for growth and change to result from the process. The therapist must enter the world of the (pre-adolescent); he cannot require (them) to function like adults in group."[11, p. 23]

Ruben is a thirteen year old boy who was referred to a group because he had no friends and was constantly scapegoated in school. Ruben's defenses included intellectualization, rationalization and isolation of affect. From time to time he would open a book and begin to read silently during group sessions. The authoritative approach led to intellectual debates between the worker and Ruben, at the expense of the others. Interpreting his behavior led only to a shrug of disinterest. Mobilizing the others to confront Ruben led to the scapegoating that he was so accustomed to. Finally, the worker created a Greek chorus out of the other members and whenever Ruben opened his book they would chant, with tongues planted firmly in cheeks, "Once again Ruben is retreating into the world of literature." This placed Ruben in a bind. The usual authoritative statement was missing, no scapegoating existed and yet something was being communicated and it short circuited Ruben's intellectual style of thinking. The collaborative "tongue in cheek" and "smile in voice" approach, coupled with a reasonable interpretation and an implicit request for him to stop reading confused Ruben and all he could do was laugh. The message which probably got through was "please join us, we like you."

In the author's experience there have been professionals who avoid working with groups of pre-adolescents. One of the more common reasons is "nothing happens that they can't get on the playground. . .I'm not a camp counselor, I'm a therapist (and I have more important things to do with my time)." Maybe so, but if the worker gives the appearance of being too sophisticated for such work, one need only look a little further to find that the real aversion is to the anxiety stimulated by the prospect of losing control in the fact of perpetual confusion. If the worker can playfully accept the kaleidoscopic nature of the pre adolescent group, the confusion will eventually be transformed into fusion (or it won't).

The Establishment of Group Rituals

Increasing the level of group distinctiveness[9, p. 148] leads to greater cohesion amongst the members. One way of fostering distinctiveness in the pre-adolescent group is through the establishment of group rituals. Ritual, although often maligned, is not merely empty, repetitive behavior. If one equates ritual with simple formality then the connotation is of an act which is superficial and lacking in depth.[12, p. 95] Rituals can best be established in groups when they occur spontaneously and with respect to mutuality.

> Ritual is concerned with relationships, either between a single individual and the supernatural, or among a group of individuals who share things together. There is something about the sharing and the expectation that makes it ritual.[12, p. 89]

The following is an example drawn from the "kittens" group which you have already been introduced to.

> One day, Diane sat in the large leather chair where the group worker usually sat. The other girls became angry and decided that they too wanted to sit in the leather chair. Rather than engaging in a power struggle we talked about the meaning of

the chair, feeling important and acting "grown up." The worker suggested that the group (including herself), take turns each week, sitting in the "big seat." This became a group ritual.

In this case the worker's thoughtful and creatively simple intervention led to a meaningful ritual, which respected the girls' passage through a new phase of development.

> The (person) who leads ritual must be something of an artist. She needs the ability of vibrating her feelings into others—call it charisma, call it empathy. . .Ritual for its own sake is vanity. Ritual for the sake of the participants reflects a thoughtfulness, a concern for others. It is easy to perform ritual for its own sake. It is more difficult to perform it for the sake of the participants.[5, p. 170]

The end of the group session is an opportune time for creating a parting ritual. In another group of ten year old girls, whose parents had been recently separated, the last five minutes of each session were reserved for passing a ball, in a circle, to one another (and the worker). This emerged after several sessions were marked by endings in which the girls either refused to leave or uncontrollably fought over a variety of objects in the room. The passing of the ball provided both an emphasis of the mutuality of the group and a symbol for loss and retrieval, not unlike the mourning process.

Another parting ritual evolved after a worker asked a group of boys, as the group was about to end, "Any famous last words?" One "wise guy" raised his finger and pursed his lips as if to prepare the others for a profound statement, and he then said "the." The others followed in suit with their own "famous last word" and a ritual was established. They ultimately decided to take turns recording the "words," which they strung into sentences, on paper. Thus the members established a ritual which allowed them to summarize their experience through a playful process of free association. It also enabled them, in a new way, to say goodbye.

Famous Last Words

Perhaps the greatest challenge in leading a pre-adolescent group is that no matter how prepared one is, one is unprepared. Your greatest ally and advisor is your creativity. The outline set forth in this paper can serve not as a bag of tricks, nor as a recipe for survival, rather as a framework within which one can create.

REFERENCE NOTES

1. Blos, P. *The Adolescent Passage: Developmental Issues.* New York: International Universities Press, Inc., 1979.
2. Castenada, C. *A Separate Reality.* New York: Pocket Books, 1974.
3. Erhard, W. "If God Had Meant Man to Fly, He Would Have Given Him Wings" (pamphlet). San Francisco, 1973.
4. Erikson, E.H. "Ontogeny of Ritualization in Man." *Philosophical Transactions of the Royal Society of London,* Series B, No. 772, Vol. CCL1, 1966, pp. 337-350.
5. Fischer, E. "Ritual as Communication." *The Roots of Ritual,* ed. J.D. Shaughnessy. Grand Rapids, Michigan: W.B. Eardmans Publ. Co., 1973, pp. 161-185.
6. Fuller, J.S. "Duo Therapy." *Journal of Child Psychiatry.* Vol. 16 No. 3, New Haven: Yale University Press, Summer, 1977, pp. 469-477.
7. Garland, J.A., Jones, H.E. and Kolodny, R.L. "A Model for Stages of Development in Social Work Groups." *Explorations in Group Work,* ed. S. Bernstein. Boston: Milford House Inc., 1973, pp. 17-71.
8. Ginott, H.G. "Innovations in Group Psychotherapy with Preadolescents." *Innovations in Group Psychotherapy,* ed. G.M. Gazda. Springfield, Illinois: Charles C. Thomas, pp. 272-294.
9. Kavanagh, A. "The Role of Ritual in Personal Development." *The Roots of Ritual,* ed. J.D. Shaughnessy. Grand Rapids, Mich.: W.B. Eerdmans Publ. Co., 1973, pp. 145-161.
10. Koestler, A. *The Act of Creation* (a study of the conscious and unconscious processes of humor, scientific discovery and art). New York: The Macmillan Co., 1964, pp. 27-101.
11. Levine, B. *Group Psychotherapy, Practice and Development.* Englewood Cliffs, N.J.: Prentice-Hall Inc., 1979, pp. 21-25.
12. Mead, M. "Ritual and Social Crisis." *The Roots of Ritual,* ed. J.D. Shaughnessy. Grand Rapids, Mich.: W.B. Eerdmans Publ. Co. 1973, pp. 87-103.
13. Redl, F. "Pre-Adolescents—What Makes Them Tick" (pamphlet). New York: Child Study Press, 1972.
14. Schwartz, W. "The Social Worker in the Group." *New Perspectives on Services to Groups.* New York: N.A.S.W., 1961.
15. Sugar, M., ed. *The Adolescent in Group and Family Therapy.* New York: Brunner/Mazel Publishers, 1975.
16. Sullivan, H.S. *The Interpersonal Theory of Psychiatry.* New York: W.W. Norton and Co. 1953, pp. 245-262.
17. Tomkins, C. *Eric Hoffer: An American Odyssey.* New York: Harper and Row Publ., 1968.
18. Watzlawick, P. *The Language of Change: Elements of Therapeutic Communication.* New York: Basic Books, Inc. 1978.
19. Yalom, I.D. *The Theory and Practice of Group Psychotherapy.* New York: Basic Books, Inc., 1975.
20. Yoshikawa, E. *Musashi.* U.S.A.: Harper and Row Publ./Kodansha Internation, 1981.

"Get'cha After School": The Professional Avoidance of Boyhood Realities

Ralph L. Kolodny

ABSTRACT. This paper points up an important aspect of latency which is much neglected in the literature of child development. The author notes the baleful effects of such neglect on the education of social workers and other professionals and on their practice with children's groups. He emphasizes the need for group workers to attend to the problems posed.

Considerable time has always been spent by social group workers in working with latency age boys. Indeed, whether in settlement house or child guidance clinic, leadership of a boys' club group has been a staple of group work practice. Social workers are asked, even exhorted, to identify with those with whom we work. Our literature and that of child psychology and psychiatry is expected to provide us with the cognitive underpinnings for the empathy that, we, hopefully, will develop for these, our young male charges. It should, therefore consider the stresses of this period as they are consciously experienced by the youngster, as he actually perceives them. Even the most clinical of social workers, those most concerned with unconscious and pre-conscious elements in human behavior, are now being urged to work "a radical transformation in the way in which clinical social work might be practiced, bringing the social worker physically and psychologically closer to the lives

Ralph L. Kolodny MA, MSSS is Professor, Boston University School of Social Work, and Visiting Professor, Ben Gurion University of Megef Beersheba, Sheva, Israel.

The author is indebted to the late Harold W. Walsh, Executive Director, Somerville-Cambridge Catholic Charitable Bureau for his assistance in developing the ideas which led to this paper.

21

of troubled people."[1] For those social workers treating or serving children of any type the literature should not confine itself to illuminating the underlying emotional challenges and tensions of latency for the male youngster, the struggle to master which takes place below the level of his conscious awareness. It must equally consider the quite conscious tensions resulting from his struggles with peers for acceptance or dominance, including those typically produced by threats to his physical well-being.

The literature upon which social workers currently rely in order to understand normal and abnormal child development and behavior does not discuss these tensions in any satisfactory manner. In it one reads a great deal about the temporary resolution of oedipal fears and jealousies and freeing up of psychic energy for the development of social skills. One finds little there, however, about those experiences of physical conflict so common to the experience of latency age males. One learns nothing from it of the fearful consternation of the ordinary latency age boy, as a peer he has somehow antagonized, hisses, "Just wait till I get ya after school!"

Physical fighting among emotionally stable boys is sometimes mentioned in this literature. Brief mention, however, is about all it does receive. Descriptions of physical conflict do appear in the classics of psychiatric group treatment for children such as the writings of Redl and Wineman and Slavson.[2] Theirs, however, was emotionally disturbed or disturbing children, boys whose fighting and whose preoccupation with physical attack one might more readily dismiss as a product of their psychopathology.

The topic of physical conflict among older latency boys is discussed in the literature on street gangs which was popular for a couple of decades. Here again, however, these were youngsters whose development had presumably been damaged by severe environmental pressures. Or in texts on childhood and youth we were told of fighting between "bullies" and "scapegoats," as if fighting occurs only between those who are maladapted, the overly aggressive or those who are not aggressive enough. Even in the instances just cited, the anguish of fighting, the pain of taking and giving blows, the ominous quality of being verbally challenged by someone who wants to hurt you, are not considered.

In his scathing article on "American Schoolrooms: Learning the Nightmare,"[3] the late Jules Henry makes us exquisitely aware of the emotional pain of latency age children subjected to the shaming devices used by classroom teachers and peers. For Henry, too, however, the world of physical pain inflicted by latency age boys on one another remains uncharted territory. That it, also, might be part of the "nightmare" is never considered.

It is as if, with the weighty attention it devotes to other material, the literature on that-which-is-to-be-expected among boys in latency is put at the service of repressing those fearful and physically painful aspects of the period which those of us who are adults would indeed like to forget. This is clearly a loss for those who would try to understand the latency experience in its fullness and to offer emotional nurture to groups of youngsters for whom it is their present reality. Even in books designed specifically to acquaint us with the way in which the child learns to interact with his social environment one finds little attention given to physical conflict as a behavioral mode. In Damon's *The Social World of the Child,* to cite a recent example, the author emphasizes that this book is about children's development of social knowledge. It concentrates not only on the child's knowledge as it is expressed verbally, but as it is manifested in the child's active dealings with his social world. Damon is interested in studying the child's social conceptions as a foundation for a description of the *child's social world* in its own terms. What he discusses is a series of empirical studies of the major social relations and social regulations in the world of the child. Yet fighting is mentioned in his book briefly and then only in the context of fighting between friends. At one point a youngster reports to the author about a classmate, Don, "who always has friends because. . .he's the best fighter." "The best fighter," he continues, always has friends. . . 'Cause if a kid beats on you, you can ask Don to beat him up and then you're not afraid of anyone in the school."[4] One would think that this kind of statement would suggest that Damon investigated the place fighting has in the lives of schoolchildren. This rich and important area, however, is left largely untouched.

With what, however, does the literature on child development in latency concern itself?

The sections on "the juvenile" in Lidz' popular text, *The Person,* for instance, cover considerable ground. Lidz directs his readers' attention to the expanding environment of the child, "the society of playmates," "the developing self concept," "the classroom as a socializing agency," "books and television," "cognitive development" and the like. When in all of this, however, Lidz writes about "new sources of anxiety and despair" he is concerned with unconscious sources. As he writes about the physical conflict which takes place during this period among children the reader obtains no idea of the anxiety or the down-right fearfulness which accompany the latency age child's immersion in the world of his peers. Lidz's breezy description of the excitement and activity of latency somehow leaves such negative affects buried and concealed from view. Lidz writes:

> As boys move beyond hide-and-seek and other games shared with girls, they rather typically play "cowboys and Indians," which will turn into "cops and robbers" and various types of military games. They have a passionate interest in marbles, kite flying, bike riding, simple ball games; and then they begin to play games such as baseball, basketball, and football with poorly organized teams, and countless fights over rules, arguments about cheating, and lopsided scores. Hours indoors are spent playing checkers, cards, and other games or in constructing models and collecting almost anything. There is the fondness for wrestling and body contact; the dares to fight, the chip on the shoulder; the avoidance of the bully, the teasing of the poor sport. There are the quarrels between friends who will never talk to one another again but seek one another out within the day. There is the boasting, the importance of winning, the complete exhaustion by bedtime. As they near the end of the period they may tend to form into larger groups that resemble gangs in order to have sufficient members to form real teams.[5]

The considerable suffering which usually accompanies the daring to fight and the chip on the shoulder, the fearful dodging in order to avoid the bully, the misery of being teased, especially by a group, do not receive even passing mention. Parents who are concerned about the negative effects of any or all of these events on their children or those of others and seek to involve themselves in such groups as Cub Scouts in order to minimize some of this are cautioned that, while sometimes their direction can be helpful:

> it is very important for peer groups to work out their own hierarchy and to set their own standards of behavior, learn to handle fights, deal with cheaters and cope with less adaptable children. It is here that children gradually work out patterns of social interaction free from adult authority. They will make mistakes but they gain essential experience.[6]

Interpersonal conflict among youngsters is assumed by Lidz to somehow contain its own satisfactory resolution. Things will work out. The usually nasty, even brutal exclusion or extrusion of the less adaptable child from his peer group, the pain of the victims of "mistakes" and the effect of these mistakes on the psychology of the victimizers are seen as marginal or incidental matters. Greater evils, presumably, will result from adult attempts to mitigate them.

Like Lidz, other writers do mention quarreling among children. Some even allude to their "cruelty." There is, however, little elaboration of this theme in their comments on the period. Again, like Lidz, these experts seem inclined to treat the fighting and cruelty like the weather, about which nothing can be done, and, therefore, little need be said beyond predicting it. The forms of physical conflict engendered by this cruelty, the psychological mechanisms used to cope emotionally with physical attack, the stress felt by the child and its influence on his subsequent functioning at school or at home, parental and sibling reactions to fighting and physical hurt, all these are barely discussed if at all. The standard psychological texts used by social workers in earlier years sometimes hinted at what might go on in regard to fighting. Cameron, for instance, mentions how the family is a safe harbor for the child when others fight him or reject him. He also describes fighting as "normal" and "common."[7] When, however, he discusses the tensions of the period and asks adults to understand what children go through, any reference to those emotional stresses engendered by the ubiquitous school-yard fist fight is conspicuous by its absence. In one of his summary paragraphs on the matter, he writes:

> The latency child must first of all move out among comparative strangers and learn to survive and enjoy himself without the protection and guidance to which he is accustomed. Within a year or two he must enter an entirely new kind of culture, the school, and diligently apply himself to concentrated learning during a six-hour day, which is almost as long as the average workingman's day. He must also continue adapting himself to the neighborhood group and his peer culture, mastering new skills, even at play, and entering into group participation with play groups whose pattern continually changes.
>
> The stresses of this phase are often overlooked by adults, who tend to idealize latency as a period of no responsibility. It is not unusual for an adult, who is himself lounging in a chair

taking his ease after seven or eight hours at work, to rebuke a child for not working harder, when the child has spent six hard hours at school and perhaps three more hard hours competing with children his own age.

The acquisition of new knowledge and new skills, at school, at play and in the home, the gaining of more and more emotional control and the entering into new role relationships, together comprise a common source of problems during the latency phase. Life between the ages of five or six and twelve or thirteen demands a great deal. In the home a child is expected to be obedient, loyal, orderly and self-controlled even when he is tired out and irritable. At school he is expected to be obedient, orderly and self-controlled, to work diligently, and to cooperate with other children or compete with them in accordance with pre-established rules. He is expected to conform to standards which he does not set, and which keep going higher and higher the older he gets.[8]

English and Pearson's *Emotional Problems of Living,* a standard text of the 1940s and one with which social work students of earlier generations were very familiar, makes no bones about the brutishness of much interpersonal interaction in latency. "During the latent period schoolchildren tend to be little bullies and tyrants. They want to control or feel they can control someone." The phenomenon of being "picked on" is prevalent. "In the latent period, when girls and boys are less supervised by older people than during the previous periods, they can be extremely cruel to each other. They form cliques and punish those they dislike by excluding them. . .it is important to them that they affect other persons and affect them rather painfully." They are also cruel to those grownups who are too weak or helpless to retaliate, as when they play pranks on older persons in the neighborhood."[9] So write English and Pearson. Their suggestions as to how to respond to this behavior center on the idea that parents "must be able to interpret to the children the reason for their cruelty and dislike of each other." The explanation to be given is that "older people have not been especially kind to the children, have not shown them the value of kindness, consideration and 'giving the other fellow a break' by example as well as by precept." They also emphasize that explanations will not "cure" all the resentment felt by the typical latency age youngster. "Something must be done about it through friendship and closer attention" in order that its emotionally corrosive effects not become irreversible.[10] The child here is considered in his role as an attacker, tyrant, bully. Nothing is said about his fears of being waylaid or tormented by his peers. But English and Pearson do call attention to the unpleasant side of latency and emphasize its importance.

In contrast, the forty years that have elapsed since English and Pearson wrote has seen this less than attractive aspect of the development of 7 to 12 year old male children in our society either ignored or underplayed. The typical reading list in a graduate school of social work course in human behavior and development provides no commentary on the painful social realities of latency for boys. The material induces little if any serious reflection on the place of physical conflict in their lives and, indeed provides students with little incentive to recollect what they once knew of these realities, as they attempt to understand the group and individual behavior of their young charges. Actually, there is no indication that authors on these reading lists feel that such matters need to be understood at all, except in perhaps the most cursory way.

It is as if an historian were to chronicle the colonial period in America while avoiding any substantial discussion of the role played by Indian warfare in the lives of the colonists, believing that his readers could grasp what life was like during this time without such knowledge. Yet those who assemble bibliographies of required and suggested readings for social work course outlines would seem to think that one can understand what life is like during latency for American boys without appreciating the place of the fist fight in their daily activities.

A perennial on such lists, to cite one example, is Erikson's *Identity: Youth and Crisis.* No current theorist equals Erikson in his ability to describe how the culture of a society and the mind and body of the individual interact to produce the unconscious tensions which fuel and give direction to behavior in children. Close consideration of the daily routine of the school age child, however, is not intended by Erikson, nor is any part of this routine examined on its own terms. It is always considered as a reflection or expression of something else.

Erikson thus never mentions the battling among boys that is a regular feature of school yard and playground life. In reading his sections on ''Childhood and the Anticipation of Roles'' and ''School Age and Task Identification'' one would not know that it exists. At one point Erikson emphasizes that ''. . .the configurations of culture and the manipulations basic to the prevailing technology must reach meaningfully into school life, supporting in every child a feeling of competence—that is, free exercise of dexterity and intelligence in the completion of serious tasks unimpaired by an infantile sense of inferiority."[11] Nowhere, however, does he discuss how physical conflict or the threat of such conflict in latency intrude on this process. Indeed, no author touches this subject in the literature to which social workers are exposed. For example, the reading on latency required of students in the basic human behavior course at the school of social work with which the present writer is most familiar appears to attach primary importance to the understanding by the student of the shifts in the direction and expression of libidinal energy which take place at this time of life. Along with this, students are given material which describes the increase in social maturity to be expected at this age.[12] Neither social work, nor any of the helping professions, seems to have considered undertaking a systematic collection of representative instances of fighting among latency age boys in their variety and detail and their examination, with a view to developing different ways to respond helpfully. Far from it. Even when the studies employed focus on observations of daily behavior, rather than on interpretations of motivation, fighting is noted briefly, but not discussed. Gesell and Ilg, their work still in use many years after its original publication, point out in one of their summary chapters on nine year olds, "Boys have considerable trouble with bullies of their own age or older."[13] In the entire 450 page book in which the behavior of children is set out in exquisite detail this is the only mention made of "bullying." This chapter is preceded by others rich in description of the child's feeling states and actions. In one of them Gesell and Ilg go on to some length enumerating the forms that the worries and apprehensions of nine year olds take.

Though Nine has few fears he is a great worrier. He is upset by little mistakes he makes. He may be apprehensive about crossing a street at a traffic light. He worries about failing in his studies; about doing the wrong thing in a social situation, such as extending his left hand instead of his right; Or not measuring up to the other children. He needs reassurance or praise, to be informed where he stands. Sometimes competition makes him worry more, and if it does it should be minimized or avoided. . . .Some nines are anxious and apprehensive about their work and about their health. They may underrate themselves as persons, lack confidence and remark,

"Oh, I am Stupid" or "I'm the dumbest." It is very important to make sure that Nine is not overplaced in regard to his school work for if he is, he will receive both his own condemnation and that of others.[14]

Nowhere in this earlier set of descriptions, however, is found any reference to that with which Gesell and Ilg later state nine year olds have considerable difficulty, namely, "bullying" by other youngsters.

The intention is not to carp at the contents of readings such as these. Their authors have a variety of aims and interests and their major theoretical and practice concerns are in some respects different from those of social group workers. One simply should realize that social work students' exposure to these readings will do little to stimulate their thinking about what the fighting and bullying so typical of the boyhood experience feels like to the participants and those close to them and what appear to be the various types of efforts by social workers to respond to the fighting, itself, and to the interaction which precedes and follows it.

This is not to say that there is nothing useful here. There is the occasional text which conveys some feeling for the knock-about world of boys in latency. For instance, if one considers the latest book describing psychoanalytic psychotherapy with latency-age children, which some social work students are called upon to read, one does catch a glimpse of this world.[15] The author, Sarnoff, discusses his views of the psychological dynamics of the stage and the proper strategies for helping emotionally disturbed children who have been unable to use the mechanisms of what Sarnoff calls "the structure of latency" to discharge drives as normal children do and, thus, to stabilize themselves. Sarnoff is clearly aware of what life can be like in latency; the stressful events of the day with which he tries to help a child deal, or the latent complexes which he attempts to help him work through, include the realities of being humiliated by peers and being pushed over and over again on the bus. Even in the case of this book, however, it is possible to come away from reading about these everyday interpersonal battles with the impression that it is only the more disturbed child who cannot adequately deal with these stressful events unaided.

The "structure of latency" of Sarnoff consists of those words and culture myths which provide pathways for the child's discharge of the normal excitements of his life. These excitements, he avers, are denied expression for long periods by teachers and parents. The child's use of the structure of latency, which operates when other pathways are blocked, harnesses his or her drives to the process of acquiring the traditions of culture. Most children, Sarnoff suggests, use fantasies to undo humiliation. The symbolic content of their fantasies ultimately shifts to signifiers whose nature is realistic and which are actually, among the cherished culture elements of a useful society. Sarnoff points out that we then do not speak of the child as fantasizing, but of his handling stress by mobilizing himself to plan for the future.[16] When he does this, the child, says Sarnoff, may be said to be in the "state of latency."

Sarnoff found that ". . . .psychopathology in latency age children reflected a failure to achieve or maintain this state of latency." In contrast, "Beyond the clinic, in placid homes and in schools, latency age children who had achieved a state of latency were to be found." He believes that, "by and large their lives are characterized by a calm."[17]

Such a characterization of latency is interesting in the light of the unmistakable, though cryptic, references to the prevalence of bullying and coercion among latency-age boys in the other texts cited above. It may lead the reader, the social work student or practitioner, either to overestimate the unusualness of an agitated response to the stress of fighting or threat of physical conflict, or to believe that severe stressors and shaky responses are largely confined to the lives of emotionally troubled children. One suspects both ideas are mistaken.

The most recent social work literature, itself, when it deals with groups for children still tiptoes around the nastier aspects of their everyday lives. Even in otherwise useful articles which offer new approaches to working with latency age youngsters who fail to meet the demands and expectations of one or another social institution— for example, those schoolchildren whom we, with sad humor, sometimes call the "recess flunkers"—the absence of any actual discussion of fist fights or similar alteracations is striking. "Teaching Children to Resolve Conflict: A Group Approach" which appeared in *Social Work* in 1981, for instance, is a lucid and helpful description of problem-solving groups for children who respond to conflict with aggression or withdrawal (and). . .never learn to resolve conflicts successfully."[18] It is also a perfect example of this form of avoidance. The author, Edleson, describes the "readiness activities" of the early meetings in these groups: playing roles, observing others making suggestions and giving feedback, and doing between meeting assignments. He spells out the skill training which follows and the final set of complex activities which is then put in place to insure that what these youngsters learned in the previous stage will be used in problem situations experienced currently and in new ones that may arise. Assignment cards requiring children to note difficulties encountered between sessions, group review of assignment cards, brainstorming, organized feedback, leader-modeling and coaching are all outlined. As part of the experience, Edleson stresses, group members even "learn how to conduct a problem-solving sequence on their own in the hope that when training ends the children will be able to assess situations and plan their resolution without assistance."[19] It seems likely that the children in these groups would bring up incidents of physical attack as problem situations and one is curious as to how these incidents are processed. In the article, however, the problem situations to which the author refers are left to our imaginations. None are described except to refer to them as "conflicts." The black eye, the bloody nose, the loosened tooth, the torn shirt, do not appear. What are set forth are techniques for discussing situations which presumably could include their occurrence.

> Training in the resolution of these problems is a multistep process. It starts with the identification of a problem situation and the generation of alternative solutions to the problem. The process continues with a discussion of the consequences of each possible solution, a selection of a solution offering the most positive result, and a modeled role-play of the selected solution by the leader. The majority of the group's time is spent in the final steps of the process in which the child who has identified a particular problem situation rehearses the modeled solution, is given an additional opportunity to incorporate this feedback into a second performance.[20]

Reading this cool description one thinks, by way of contrast, of Russell Baker's evocative memoir, *Growing Up.* As an eleven year older Baker used to skate up to a hilltop that looked far out over the Hackensack, New Jersey meadows. In one passage he describes how he "loved to sit and stare at that fantasy (New York) rising miles and miles away through the mist." He then adds, almost casually, "I was sitting there day dreaming late one autumn afternoon when Walter came along to beat me up. I had been beaten up three or four times by Walter for not being Irish.''[21]

One cannot help but mark the emotional distance between the neatly organized discussion of the handling of conflict by Edelson and the welter of feelings aroused by the reality of a physical attack such as that described by Baker.

Mental health and social science professionals tend to write of latency as if affected by selective amnesia, forgetting the pain that normally characterizes interaction among boys during this time of their lives. Oddly enough, the work of the imaginative journalist or novelist often provides a more accurate picture. Compare the comments made by the psychologist authors of a recent treatise on childhood with the description Ray Bradbury, dean of American social science fantasy writers, offers of the same period.

Psychologists Stone and Church, in their book, write of the difficulties of latency in almost rollicking fashion. The frightening aspect of behavior such as scapegoating or being scapegoated is sealed over as these authors treat us to a bit of unsubstantiated, but generally accepted, social psychological folklore.

> The gang, too, has its set of labels by which it knows the child and he knows himself. The gang is quick to seize on any idiosyncrasy of constitution, manner, skill, or whatever, and thereafter to treat the child in terms of this trait. The stereotype which the gang holds of the child is often expressed in his nickname; Skinny, Fatso, Four-eyes, Dopey, Professor, Limpy—the total frankness, especially of boys, often startles adults. Most children wear their nicknames proudly, even opprobrious ones, as a badge of their belonging, of having an identity for the group. Any recognition, even contempt or mockery, is preferable to being ignored. Even the outcast or scapegoat would rather have the gang persecute him than act as if he didn't exist, and even the label ''Stinky'' means that he has an identity.[22]

One cannot, of course, help but wonder how many serious studies have been conducted of youngsters' feelings about being called ''Stinky,'' in preference to being ignored.

Ray Bradbury will have none of any prettying up of these meaner aspects of latency. Bradbury's imaginary world comes closer to the actual world in which professional helpers find themselves when they work with or treat latency age boys than the pallid imitation of life offered in the professional literature. In the latter, somehow, the pain of being chased is always compensated for by the fun of running.

In one of his fantasies Bradbury creates a situation in which a recently widowed young father, Underhill, confronts the reality of the local playground. The similarity between the violent behavior he observes there and the memories of his own childhood overwhelms him, so much so that he makes a pact with the Mephistopholean figure who manages the playground. Their agreement involves Underhill becoming a child again. He enters the playground in his son's stead, while his son takes over his body and his place in the adult world.

From the outset the story assaults the reader with the sounds and smells of latency.

> Now (Underhill) saw the children! They were dashing across the playground meadow, fighting, pummeling, scratching, falling, every wound bleeding or about to bleed or freshly caked over. A dozen cats thrown among sleeping dogs could not have shrieked as loud. With incredible clarity, Mr. Underhill saw the tiniest cuts and scabs on knees and faces. . . .He sniffed the cutting odors of salve, raw adhesive, camphor and pink Mercurochrome, so strong it lay bitter on his tongue. An iodine wind blew through the steel fence wires which glinted dully in the gray light of the overcast day. The rushing children were hell cut loose in a vast pinball table, colliding, and banging, and totaling of hits and misses, thrusts and plungings to a grand and as yet unforeseen total of brutalities.[24]

Underhill stands bemused. He is clear, however, about the meaning of what he sees.

> Now the Playground was an immense iron industry whose sole products were pain, sadism, and sorrow. If you watched half an hour there wasn't a face in the entire enclosure that didn't wince, cry, redden with anger, pale with fear, one moment or another. Really! Who said childhood was the best time of life? When in reality it was the most terrible, the most merciless era, the barbaric time when there were no police to protect you, only parents preoccupied with themselves and their taller world.[25]

Carol, Underhill's sister, chides him for his "exaggerated" response to what he observes. All boys she suggests, have to "take a little beating" and "beat up others." Underhill rejects this complacent attitude.

> But Carol didn't give you a chance, damn it! She wanted the boy put in a vise and squashed. She wanted him reamed and punctured and given the laying on of hands. To be beaten from playground to kindergarten, to grammar school, to junior high to high school. If he was lucky, in high school the beatings and sadisms would refine themselves, the sea of blood and spittle would drain back down the shore of years and Jim would be left upon the edge of maturity, with God knows what outlook to the future.[26]

To top it all off, much of the violence, Underhill remembers, is impersonal. The child's persecutor may very well be someone he doesn't know.

> How ingenious, the cold, deep Playground. You never knew where anyone lived. The boy who knocked your teeth out, who was *he?* Nobody knew. Why, you could come here one day, beat the living tar out of some smaller child, and run on the next day to some *other* playground. They would never find you.[27]

Some kind of compromise has to be made, of course. One cannot change the facts of life. Still, one cannot help but be troubled by them.

> He knew Carol was right, of course. This was the world, you lived in it. You accepted it. But that was the very trouble! He had been through the mill already, he knew what it was to be a boy among lions, his own childhood had come rushing back to him in the last few hours, a time of terror and violence, and now he could not bear to think of Jim's going through it all those long years[28]

This is Bradbury's view of latency, his unvarnished truth about childhood, unconcealed by the protective haze of time and the emotional neutrality of the professional text. Bradbury's story does not suggest to the social worker what he should do "on the playground." It certainly prepares him, however, for the emotional climate of children's groups and for what he will encounter if he works with groups of boys for anything beyond a few weeks.

There have been times in the history of social group work when we have described what we have tried to do to help children manage themselves in this hurly burly of interaction, of attack and counterattack, of scapegoating and flight. One sees evidence of this in the articles on scapegoating by Shulman, Wineman and others, and in the writer's discussion some years ago of the impact of peer group activities on the isolated child.[29] We need many more such descriptions, however, of "combat" situations, of child behavior and worker efforts with all sorts of youngsters, whether normal or emotionally disturbed. Only in this way can we systematically study such situations and behavior and begin to teach ourselves and our students and supervisees about helping children to handle the realities of boyhood. To be frank, what social work, psychology and psychiatry presently offer by way of professional responses to fighting among boys in groups are alibis for neutrality and inaction on the one hand, and harshness in the guise of firmness on the other.

Prescriptions for responses will come later. What is most needed now is an unfettered view of the painful nature of much of the social life of boys of grade school age and well-developed descriptions of how this is manifested. Redl has spoken, in his gentle, jesting way, of workers in their "daily warfare with children." The field of social work needs regular, thorough and detailed descriptions from workers of "daily warfare among children." Perhaps then we can move toward contributing to its amelioration, or, at least, can respond, more directly and helpfully to its casualties.

In doing this we, as social workers, will have to rely mainly on ourselves rather than on the literature of the sister disciplines to which we are accustomed to turn for our fundamental ideas. In regard to psychoanalytic theory, for example, Lidz has pointed out that ". . .the juvenile period has received little attention in classic psychoanalytic developmental theory, and few aside from Sullivan and educational psychologists have emphasized its importance.[30] Even when theorists of this orientation do attend to latency issues their suggestions regarding the fighting which is rife among boys in latency are, as we have seen, less than satisfying. It is worth noting, for example, that in Gardner's chapter on the juvenile years, in sixty one pages of recorded dialogue with parents, fighting is covered in one paragraph. Responding to a mother's question, the psychiatrist-author says:

Children often do learn the sad effects of cruelty at the hands of other children. They learn the physical discomfort dealt them by the bully—and they experience feelings of depression and frustration generated by the derogatory remarks of their companions who taunt them over a million things. I'm afraid the pain and anxiety resulting from these physical and verbal abuses go far to strengthen their own impulses to be cruel. Whenever an episode of this kind occurs to them, it is helpful if the parents underline the ill effects that cruelty has. When a child is cruel he should be reminded of how he felt in a similar circumstance. His behavior should not be allowed to go unchallenged. One of the best opportunities that a parent has, of course, to teach kindness is by his own conduct. Children are very aware of the way their parents behave not only toward them but also toward those around them.[31]

Clearly the matter calls for a much more extensive presentation and useful response than Gardner seems able to offer. The challenge to group workers is to develop such responses. To be sure, as someone has said in connection with a social psychological issue of another sort, "merely recognizing this challenge will not enable us to meet it, but recognizing it is where we must begin."[32]

NOTES

1. Harry Wasserman, "Reflections on Clinical Social Work," *Smith College Studies in Social Work*, Vol. LII, No. 3, June, 1982, p. 184.

2. Fritz Redl and David Wineman, *Children Who Hate*, The Free Press, Glencoe, Illinois, 1949 and S.R. Slavson, *Introduction to Group Therapy*, International Universities Press, New York, 1943.

3. Jules Henry, "American Schoolrooms; Learning the Nightmare," *Columbia University Forum*, Vol II, No.2, Spring, 1963, pp.24-30.

4. William Damon, *The Social World of the Child*, Jossey Bass, San Francisco, 1977, p. 159.

5. Theodore Lidz, *The Person*, Basic Books, N.Y., 1976, p.281.

6. *Ibid*, p. 282.

7. Norman Cameron, *Personality Development and Psychopathology*, Houghton, Mifflin, and Co., Boston, 1963, pp. 78-81.

8. *Ibid*, pp. 83-84.

9. O.S. English and G.H.J. Pearson, Emotional Problems of Living, WW Norton and Co., 1945, p. 137.

10. *Ibid*, p. 138.

11. Erik Erikson, *Identity: Youth and Crisis,* WW Norton Co., NY, 1968, P. 126.

12. The required reading includes, Berta Bornstein, "On Latency" *Psychoanalytic Study of the Child,* Volume Six, Yale University Press, New Haven, 1951, pp. 279-285, Arnold Gesell and Frances Ilg, *The Child from Five to Ten,* Harper and Bros., New York, 1946, George Gardner, "The Balanced Expression of Oedipal Remnants," *Smith College Studies in Social Work,* Volume 27, No. 3, June, 1957, pp. 188-210, and Lili Peller, "Libidinal Phases, Ego Development and Play," *Psychoanalytic Study of the Child,* Volume Nine, Yale University Press, New Haven, 1954, pp. 178-198.

13. Gesell and Ilg, *op.cit.,* pp. 202-203.

14. *Ibid,* p. 356.

15. Charles Sarnoff, *Latency,* Jason Aronson, New York, 1976.

16. *Ibid,* pp. 11-14.

17. *Ibid,* p. 6.

18. Jeffrey L. Edelson, "Teaching Children to Resolve Conflict: A Group Approach," *Social Work,* Vol. 26, No. 6, November, 1981, pp. 488-493.

19. *Ibid,* p. 491.

20. *Idem.*

21. Russell Baker, *Growing Up,* Congdon and Weed, New York, 1982, p. 124.

22. L. Joseph Stone and Joseph Church, *Childhood and Adolescence,* Random House, New York, 1968, p. 371.

23. Ray Bradbury, "The Playground," *Fahrenheit 451,* Ray Bradbury, editor, Simon and Schuster, New York, 1967.

24. *Ibid,* pp. 151-152.

25. *Ibid,* p. 153.

26. *Ibid,* p. 159.

27. *Ibid,* p. 161.

28. *Ibid,* p. 160

29. Lawrence Shulman, "Scapegoats, Group Workers and Pre-emptive Intervention," *Social Work,* Vol. 12, No. 2, April, 1967, pp. 37-43, David Wineman, "The Life Space Interview," *Social Work,* Vol. 4, No. 1, January, 1959, p. 10, James Garland and Ralph Kolodny, "Characteristics and Resolution of Scapegoating" *Social Work Practice 1967,* Columbia University Press, New York, 1967, and Ralph Kolodny, "The Impact of Peer Group Activity on the Isolated Child," *Smith College Studies in Social Work,* Vol. 37, No. 1, February, 1967, pp. 142-158.

30. Lidz, *op. cit.,* p. 277.

31. George Gardner, *The Emerging Personality,* Delacorte Press, New York, 1970, p. 127.

32. Michael Doyle, "Why Democracies are Prone to Fight Dictators," *The Wall Street Journal,* August 25, 1983, p. 18.

Call for Papers

Contributions are invited for a special issue of *Social Work with Groups*. The special issue is to appear in the Fall of 1986 and will be devoted entirely to research in group work. Special guest editor will be Ronald A. Feldman of Washington University, St. Louis. Associate guest editors are Larry E. Davis, (Washington University, St. Louis), Maeda Galinsky (University of North Carolina, Chapel Hill), Sheldon D. Rose (University of Wisconsin, Madison), Martin Sundel (University of Texas, Arlington) and James K. Whittaker (University of Washington, Seattle).

Consideration will be given to research reports, evaluations of group work programs, synthesis of research concerning pertinent practice topics, discussions of research advances or methodological issues, operationalization of dependent and independent variables in group work practice or research, the study of group developmental processes, and analyses of measurement issues or techniques. Original papers on any and all aspects of group work research are welcome.

All manuscripts should conform to the requirements of manuscripts for *Social Work with Groups*. Papers can be submitted to the Special Editor for this issue at The George Warren Brown School of Social Work, Washington University, St. Louis, Missouri 63130. While the deadline for submission is March 1, 1985, manuscripts will be welcome in advance of that date.

Peer Culture and the Organization of Self and Object Representations in Children's Psychotherapy Groups

Gary D. Pfeifer
Deborah Weinstock-Savoy

ABSTRACT. In the article which follows the authors explore the significance of children's peer culture and its implications for therapeutic activity on the part of the group worker. A review of the theoretical formulations of leading thinkers in the field forms the backdrop for the authors' discussion of their own work with treatment groups for children. This discussion features a description of their approach to creating a peer culture which allows members to develop relationships and a cohesive sense of self.

Introduction

This paper will begin to explicate the significance of culture as a variable in group psychotherapy for children. We are particularly interested in exploring the following questions: (1) How does "peer culture"—which forms indigenously within children's psychotherapy groups as well as other arenas within which children congregate—function as a "curative factor" (Yalom, 1975) in children's group psychotherapy? (2) How does peer culture provide the therapist with a point of access to the psychosocial (Erikson, 1952) and

Gary Pfeifer, PhD, is an Instructor of Psychology in the Department of Psychiatry, Harvard Medical School and Director Children's Clinical Services at Brookline Mental Health Center. Deborah Weinstock-Savoy is a Clinical Fellow in Psychology in the Department of Psychiatry, Harvard Medical School and a Doctoral Candidate in Clinical Psychology at Boston University.

We wish to thank our colleagues at the Brookline Mental Health Center, especially James Caron, Martha Markowitz and David Spinner, for their collaborative support in the preparation of this paper. The authors take full responsibility for the final draft.

39

representational (Sandler and Rosenblatt, 1962) worlds of his/her clients? (3) How and when can the development of peer culture be influenced by the therapist with reference to particular therapeutic goals?

Before pursuing our specific topic further, we will briefly review some of the more fundamental ideas addressed by leading figures in the field of children's group therapy over the last half century. This review is by no means comprehensive but rather will highlight some significant historical trends associated with outpatient groups for children.

The most thoroughly explicated forms of children's group psychotherapy were developed by S.R. Slavson and his colleagues at the Jewish Board of Guardians in New York City (Slavson, 1945, 1959, 1964; Gabriel, 1937). Perhaps the best known form, activity group therapy (Scheidlinger 1947) was based on the assumption that therapeutic change occurred through an emotionally corrective experience resulting from the convergence of three key elements: (1) a conditioned environment; (2) a well balanced group composition; and (3) a neutral though accepting therapist (Slavson and Schiffer, 1975). In activity group therapy, treatment was described as occurring "through the group," i.e., as a result of children's complementary adaptive styles balancing one another within the free but safe environment created and maintained by the group therapist. The therapist rarely intervened physically or verbally but rather would subtly regulate interaction when necessary by adjusting his or her proximity to the children and manipulating objects in the room (Schiffer, 1952). Children were carefully screened prior to placement, and this form of treatment was not recommended for children with "serious neurotic problems" or worse.

Another form of group treatment developed by Slavson et al. was called *activity interview therapy*. While similar to the activity groups in several ways, this treatment "in the group" depended heavily upon the therapist making clarifying and interpretive statements to individuals or subgroups during the course of regular activity. Children with serious neurotic symptomology were referred to these groups, and because treatment depended heavily upon verbal interaction between therapist and child, less emphasis was placed on achieving a perfectly balanced group composition.

Finally, Slavson and Shiffer (1975) describe *play group therapy* as the treatment of choice for prelatency children. This form of treatment was conducted in a well equipped playroom filled with standard fantasy materials such as clay, dolls and puppets. Children's play was interpreted as the therapist observed and interacted with each child individually and in subgroups (Schiffer, 1969). None of the above treatment approaches were recommended for psychotic or severely disturbed (borderline) children; nor for children with serious impulse disorders (Slavson, 1955).

Ginott (1961) outlined a model similar to activity group therapy but placing greater emphasis upon the therapeutic significance of the group setting per se. He noted that the group context provided the opportunity for each child to experience peer acceptance and to form healthy identifications growing out of multilateral relationships. In describing the unique advantages of groups, he emphasized the therapeutic significance of reciprocity, which, he believed, was not possible in the one-to-one therapeutic relationship. He argued that mutual stimulation of ideas and feelings in group can foster insight; furthermore children are forced, in groups, to reevaluate their behavior in the light of peer interaction. Thus group was believed to augment the opportunity for reality testing and provide an opportunity for children to learn more adaptive interpersonal skills.

Over the past decade, advancements in ego psychological theory, and the mandate for public agencies to treat an increasingly disturbed population of children, have led to modifications in these classical activity and play therapy group models. Authors such as Scheidlinger (1965, 1977) Schamess (1976) and Frank (1976) have reviewed various diverse models for treating ego-impaired children in outpatient settings. Of particular interest are the ego developmental models proposed by Schamess (1976) and Frank (1976) which place considerably less emphasis upon the "conditioned environment" and "group composition" than do the classical models of Slavson et al. They rather emphasize the active intervention of the therapist who in setting firm limits encourages children to verbalize rather than act upon feelings. In such groups the therapist operates as an auxiliary ego and encourages children's identification with his or her soothing and organizing functions. Through verbalizing affects children become able to tolerate greater degrees of separation and individualization (Frank, 1983; Mahler, Pine and Bergman, 1975).

It is of interest to note that these psychoanalytically-informed approaches to treating children in groups have tended to emphasize the psychodynamics of the individual child more than group process per se. The tradition of social group work practice, in contrast, draws upon a broader sociological perspective. It assumes that basic interdependence of individual and group, and the normative importance of group affiliation as an essential human need.

Out of this tradition has come a variety of important concepts and emphases, including the significance of group cohesion, patterns of communication, problem-solving, and modes of group functioning (instrumental and expressive) (Papell and Rothman, 1980). Also alluded to is a concept of culture, which is defined both in terms of the varied norms and values that individuals bring to group, and the shared traditions and meanings that develop within a given group (Wilson and Ryland, 1981).

Grounded in the social group work approach, the work of Garland, Jones, Kolodny, and their collaborators at Boston University pays special attention to group process in outlining five stages of development applicable to childrens' psychotherapy groups. The stages:

1. preaffiliation
2. power and control
3. intimacy
4. differentiation
5. separation

provide useful guidelines for tracing the natural developmental history of particular children's therapy groups.[1]

In attempting to integrate the perspectives of social group work and psychoanalytically-oriented children's group psychotherapy, the concept of culture may provide a crucial bridge, a way of relating the development of the group as a whole with that of the individual. Indeed, it might be proposed that culture provides the matrix for the simultaneous organization of experience within the group and within the developing ego of each child. Herein lies one of the most powerful arguments for choosing group therapy as a treatment modality for children.

---

[1]The development of group culture discussed at length in an earlier version of this paper (Pfeifer and Weinstock-Savoy, 1982) presented at the Fifth Annual Conference of the Children's Group Therapy Association has been/will be published separately under the title "Group Culture and the Natural History of a Boys Psychotherapy Group" (Pfeifer and Weinstock-Savoy, 1984).

A Concept of Group Culture

The concept of culture employed in this paper draws upon both psychoanalytic and modern ethnographic theory. The definition of culture which we find most parsimonious and most clinically useful is that proposed by Clifford Geertz (1975) in the introductory chapter to his *Interpretations of Culture.* Following Max Weber, Geertz metaphorically describes "man" as "an animal suspended in webs of significance which he himself has spun"; culture, Geertz continues, is the webwork, and its analysis an interpretive science devoted to tracing and understanding connection in context. Because culture is a network of meanings, it may only be grasped through what Geertz refers to as the "thick description" of the native's point of view.[2]

This simple yet widereaching definition of culture parallels at interpersonal and societal levels of analysis, broad lines of psychological development which have been at the pinnacle of theoretical interest among contemporary psychoanalytically-oriented thinkers. Essentially, culture may be thought to organize self and object representations among human beings living in groups. Thus the culture concept may be particularly relevant to understanding aspects of the development of narcissism (Kohut 1971, 1977) and various lines of ego functioning such as object relations, affect regulation, integration and synthesis.

Winnicott (1967) has addressed the question of the psychological significance of culture and has theoretically located culture in the realm of transitional phenomena; culture symbolically and functionally represents the interplay between separateness and union. While acknowledging that culture exists in a common pool, into which individuals contribute and from which they draw, Winnicott argues that culture must be experienced by each individual as self-created. As "webs of significance," then, culture can not be simply adopted as learned but must rather be created—spun, as it were—by the individual striving to become connected with the world around. Thus, this webwork, which Geertz has called culture, for Winnicott

---

[2]It is of interest to note that an important methodological parallel has been drawn by some contemporary psychological anthropologists (Levine, 1971, 1973; Levine and Pfeifer, 1982) between this form of ethnographic description—compiled by an ethnographer and his or her informants over a period of many months through intensive daily field research—and the practice of a psychoanalyst and analysand creating the latters personal life history through repeated observations during the treatment process.

spans —and indeed connects—the space between self and environment, i.e., the world of transitional phenomena.

Erik Erikson has probably added more to our appreciation of the role of cultural context in the development of the synthetic function of the ego than any other ego-psychological theorist. In *Childhood and Society,* Erikson describes the relationship between the two as "the way in which the ego's synthesis grows—or fails to grow—out of the soil of social organization" (1963, p. 282).

The contributions of Erikson most relevant to the present discussion are: the concept of group identity, what he defines as a group's basic ways of organizing experience; and his seminal concept of ego identity, which he defines as "the accrued experience of the ego's ability to integrate all identifications with the vicissitudes of the libido, with the aptitudes developed out of endowment, and with the opportunities offered in social roles" (1963, p. 261).

The last part of the definition—the ego's ability to integrate identifications with the opportunities offered in social roles—makes clear that the concept of ego identity is thoroughly embedded within a social context.

Erikson expands this theme in the following quote:

> A child who has just found himself able to walk seems not only driven to repeat and to perfect the act of walking by libidinal pleasure in the sense of Freud's locomotor eroticism; or by the need for mastery in the sense of Ives Hendrik's work principle; he also becomes aware of the new status and stature of "he who can walk", with whatever connotations this happens to have in the coordinates of his culture's life plan—be it "he who will go far," or "he who will be upright," or "he who might go too far." To be "one who can walk" becomes one of the many steps in child development which through the coincidence of physical mastery and cultural meaning, of functional pleasure and social recognition, contribute to a more realistic self-esteem. By no means only a narcissistic corroboration of infantile omnipotence (that can be had more cheaply), this self-esteem grows to be a conviction that the ego is learning effective steps towards a tangible collective future, that it is developing into a defined ego within a social context. This sense I wish to call *ego identity.* (Erikson, 1980, p. 22)

Erikson goes on to say that such complementarity of ego synthesis and social organization provides the growing child with a "vitalizing sense of reality from the awareness that his individual way of mastering experience (his ego synthesis) is a successful variant of a group identity" (p. 21). In slightly different language, we would say that a child's ability to tap into the shared meanings of his or her social group enlarges and enriches his or her sense of meaning and worth.

Grunebaum and Solomon (1980, 1982) provide a different but complementary perspective on the importance of the peer group context for individual development. Following Anna Freud (1962), they suggest a focus on peer relatedness as a developmental line in and of itself.

Grunebaum and Solomon predict that the developmental phases of a peer-oriented psychotherapy group (with adults) will recapitulate the child's progression along the developmental line of peer relatedness, moving from a parent-child focus to a focus on relationships to peers. "As a group member, an individual would move from a primitive attachment to the group leader, then to superficial unstable aggregates, towards *an identification of self with a cohesive, stable, differentiated group culture.*" (1982, p. 300, emphasis added)

They make the point that the age of the children involved, and/or the stage of peer relatedness achieved by the individual members (whether adults or children), will affect the kind of group culture that would develop, and the leader's role must vary accordingly. "The mother supervising several two-year olds in a play group, the nursery school teacher, the classroom teacher of latency-aged and older children, the coach of teams of different ages, and the camp counselor, all have radically different tasks to accomplish. The same must be true of group psychotherapists" (1982, p. 302).

Applying the concept of culture as a self created though shared organizing system of meanings, to the world of children's group psychotherapy, we will distinguish between indigenous peer culture and therapeutic group culture. *Indigenous peer culture* refers to the natural organization of meanings created and maintained by a given cohort of children interacting and communicating among one another within the context of frequented arenas of action. Furthermore, indigenous peer group culture, specifically, organizes those phenomena which are salient to the developmental level and sociohistorical context of a *given* cohort of children.

Therapeutic group culture refers to the particular network of meanings established during the course of a given psychotherapy group. These meanings are often organized around the particular maladaptions with which children are referred for treatment, such as pathogenic self and object representations that interfere with adaptive social functioning. To the extent that children are capable of assimilating indigenous peer culture it may become the common ground for interaction within the therapy group. Parenthetically, the ease with which children beginning psychotherapy groups are able to employ indigenous peer culture is a good diagnostic indicator of their relative self and ego development.

A function of therapeutic group culture to be highlighted below involves the regulation of affect around salient self and object representations which are repeatedly revealed to group members through a variety of media.

The Emergence of Peer Culture in a Group of Ego-Impaired Boys

A concrete example may be clarifying at this point.

A group of mostly disadvantaged, ego-impaired boys was formed at the request of their school guidance counselor toward the second half of their first grade year. These boys were described by teachers as overly aggressive and disruptive in the classroom. Unable to engage in any organized activity, they would essentially run amok during early group sessions, constantly testing limits and expressing overwhelmingly angry affect toward each other, the therapists and other objects. After a brief period in a rather inadequate group room at the school, the boys would explode out the door onto the playground where they would continue to have difficulty regulating their affects and controlling their behavior.

Most of these boys entered group with damaged egos and were thus unable to embrace or create a functional indigenous peer culture even to the limited extent that might be available to them given their chronological age, i.e., relationships based on mutual interest in activities, or even mere proximity. While they shared some explicit meanings with reference to such salient themes as masculinity, authority, goodness and badness, their underdeveloped ability to integrate symbols left them affectively overwhelmed and out of control. The initially unstructured setting of the group was not helpful to them as they were incapable of creating their own organization.

After several months the group began to make weekly excursions to the small 19th century cemetery across the street from school.

Here the boys periodically engaged the therapists in reading grave-stones and more frequently in a spontaneously-evolved game of "hide and seek tag" (during which the boys would run and hide and the therapists were expected to catch them). They seemed to find this setting and their activities personally soothing and conducive to group cohesiveness in a way that no former activity had been. During this period they began to talk about the purpose of the group and one child, questioning why a quiet withdrawn boy had been included, labled it "the group for bad boys."

This cemetery period marked the initial emergence of functional indigenous peer culture into "the group for bad boys." The boys used common meanings associated with the setting to begin to master their intense anxieties. They assigned roles to the therapists which allowed them to be used as sources of both learning and gratification while at the same time retaining their then necessarily negative transferential meaning as dangerous objects to be avoided, taunted and feared. Thus embodying these contrasting object representations through common elements of the boys' transferences, the therapists were essential to the manner in which the boys began to organize self-representations within the group. Cast in this strategic position the therapists were able to begin constructing a therapeutic group culture through verbalization, where previously they had only been able to set physical limits and then not always successfully.

After several months the group was banned from the cemetery. A friendly policeman, who despite acknowledging that the boys had really done nothing wrong, nevertheless had to carry out his duty and enforce the law after neighbors had complained. Interestingly, the boys, who routinely disobeyed rules, never returned to the cemetery. They did, however, regress during varied activities which they were free to choose from a wide assortment of options. At this point the co-therapists agreed to use some of their recently-won, but rapidly diminishing leverage, and decide the weekly activity for the group (in fact with such ego-impaired children this would have been appropriate from the beginning). One common choice which was quite literally palatable to the boys, was to go out for pizza.

Toward the end of their 2nd grade year (about a year and a quarter into the group) the boys began to show an interest in the computer games at the local pizzeria where they occasionally went for an outing. While all were relatively unskilled at the games, they nonetheless played enthusiastically, cheered one another on, watched the more achieved older players with awe and admiration and encouraged the male co-therapist to try the games, displaying their first unambivalent, positive identification with him.

This marked a substantial strengthening of the therapeutic group culture which became possible through the boys embracing a very salient set of symbols operating in contemporary indigenous peer culture.

An Ethnographic Digression

Indeed, the interest of the group for bad boys' in computer video games is quite normative for boys from early latency into adolescence in the greater Boston area during the early 1980s and a brief digression into suburban ethnography may be useful here.

The activity "playing video games" taps and provides an organizational context for a variety of commonly observable developmental issues including: mastery-competence strivings, masculine identification, concern with potency, learning social conventions around sharing and turn taking, and sublimation of aggression and self control. Anyone who has frequented a video games site— from the corner laundromat to an elaborate arcade—cannot help but notice the utter seriousness with which children (primarily boys) learn and adhere to social conventions around play. Special characteristics of indigenous peer culture with reference to video games involve the respected autonomy of the player and neutrality of the computer itself. While 5 boys, just watching or awaiting their turn, may observe another play a game for several minutes, it is rare that a poor showing will be greeted with snickers or taunts. Indeed, in contrast to other settings, while a particularly competent performance may be verbally recognized, a poor performer will be either politely ignored or perhaps given concrete advice for self improvement. During direct competition (2 player games) dispute is rare; while one may bemoan a bad break, the judgment of the machine is final. Furthermore, it is not unusual for a player to verbally support his "opponent's" performance against the computer. The intervention of the machine creates both a common adversary and a referee. Competition occurs but tends to be defined more as parallel tests of personal excellence rather than a win or lose situation. Getting back to the psychotherapy group briefly described above, a few points are worth noting. For this group (as well as others in which the first author has participated) the video arcade provides both an organization and a metaphor for working through some of the most fundamental issues for which children are referred for psychotherapy. Each boy, in the clear view of his peers, according to rules and with reference to the meanings they all share, strives for self-improvement. The score a boy achieves in a given game is not in itself important. The fact that, in a context that all value, he works toward self-improvement while others watch—sometimes empathically, sometimes not and that he, for the moment, is the one in control—*is* of therapeutic significance. Furthermore, through this or any repeated activity, a consistent arena is created within which the therapist may identify, clarify and at times interpret salient affects and meanings. Thus, culture provides structure, and allows the therapist substantially more latitude to address issues that might otherwise remain inaccessible.

Converging Individual and Collective Self-Representation in a Group of Narcissisticly Impaired Boys

A remarkable quality of peer culture—indigenous or specifically therapeutic—is its propensity to organize, simultaneously, diverse individual as well as collective meanings within a single symbolic arena. In this way a well-functioning peer culture has the potential to allow each group member the experience of sameness and difference which is so fundamental to developing relationships and a cohesive sense of self. When children enter a group with serious impairment along particular lines of development, their ability to tap this dimension of indigenous peer culture may be impeded. For such children, a psychotherapy group, with its "self-consciously" accepting and flexible culture, fostered by the therapist(s), may provide an opportunity for acculturation which might otherwise be impossible. Thus by expanding the limits of acceptable difference (e.g., the therapist saying, "you are all welcome in this group even if you can't always understand each other") and by highlighting salient commonalities which may be atypical to indigenous groupings (e.g., a member saying "we're all in this boys' group because we all have trouble making friends"), therapeutic group culture provides for each individual a framework for integrating previously split-off self-representations. Consider the following clinical vignette.

At the request of the guidance counselor, a group of fourth and fifth grade boys was formed at a local school. While from diverse family backgrounds each boy, for reasons clearly understandable within the context of his personal history, suffered from chronically low self esteem and displayed relatively poor peer interactive skills. Although each of the boys was subject to some level of ego-impairment, they were all socially hungry, able to regulate affect to a reasonable extent and none would be considered within the borderline range. The group was led by male cotherapists and met weekly during school time in the guidance counselor's suite, the school playground or gymnasium. The group, which over two years had rarely been chaotic, was immediately cohesive, usually agreeing upon a weekly activity in which everyone including the adults was expected to and did participate. During the first session one boy, Brian (who had recently moved to Brookline) introduced an interactive fantasy game which he called "statues." The game consisted of one boy playing the role of storekeeper and another, the customer, negotiating over the sale of statues—everyone else—which, when switched on would perform random activities, each at his own discretion.

During the earliest meetings of "boys' group," as it became known by the members, a therapeutic group culture was spontaneously created by the members (an occurrence perhaps attributable to the relative ego strength of each boy as well as to the particular composition of the group) and was displayed for all to see through the statue game. Many themes revealed through the game had clear collective salience: each statue when switched on revealed some self-representation of the boy playing the role, which was being presented for acceptance. Whether demonstrating systematic work behavior, wild and awkward acrobatics, lethargy or rage, a common wish of each boy playing statues was to be "bought." While this wish was collectively held, the specific self-representations being presented for sale were as unique as the history of each participant. During the early months of boys' group, significant features of each boy's damaged self were revealed by his statue when switched on, but receded behind a stone face when the statue was switched off again. Brian, the game's originator, was an affectionate statue, aiming to please, whose need for physical contact and love, however, led him to flop incompetently all over the others (especially the two therapists). Ken, a depressed South American boy separated from mother during early childhood, would sometimes fall over on his side and other times become a primitive monster who needed to be kept in a separate room from the others. Alan, an upper middle class boy whose early bout with leukemia had left him developmentally delayed though not apparently damaged, would imitate what the others had done two weeks before. Sid, whose mother had been preoccupied with the slow death of her father during the boy's early childhood, presented as a stiff compliant statue who occasionally mimicked the others' aggressive postures, but without conviction. Finally Randy, a deprived, biracial boy from a large chaotic family, presented as a cool macho statue which quickly became the ideal of the entire group. Indeed, the extent to which Randy's grandiose self presentation became an organizer—a sort of grandiose self object—for the beleagured self-representations of this group of narcissticly injured boys is best illustrated later in the group when the activity shifted to kickball.

Like statues, kickball was an activity which simultaneously organized the member's collective and individual self-representations. A stronger element of indigenous peer culture was introduced in the kickball game, for here such social inevitables as competition, competence and cooperation were involved. The repeated games were organized by rules and conventions common to the school playground with one noticeable exception: no one kept score. This is not to say that no one noticed or was accountable for the quality of play. On the contrary, each boy worked to be a star, trying to kick homeruns, to dodge thrown balls and making attempts at diving catches. Only one boy, however, Randy, possessed the physical talent and skill to do so. A clear status hierarchy formed in the group, which was revealed on the kickball field. Randy was admired by all, and though his "selfish" exhibitionistic play often cost his team as many runs as he scored, no one criticized him (except the co-therapists who, confusing their roles with those of a coach at times had difficulty with a variety of intense countertransference feelings elicited by Randy). The groups collective identification with Randy's grandiose self-presentation was perfectly clear for months but became even more striking through unanimous verbalization when Randy, due to a scheduling conflict with a new special education class, was forced to leave the group. Randy's departure led to the boys' expressing intense anger, sadness, and confusion, and to a reorganization of self-presentations. On the one hand, they complained; "The group's not the same without Randy; you made him leave! It's boring; why did he have to go?" On the other hand, with the embodiment of their grandiose self absent, the status heirarchy—geared as it was around the organization of narcissistic self-representations—was thrown into flux. Each boy knew where he had been; Brian, the second-strongest announced in a tough voice "I'm Randy now!" Ken announced "Then I'm Brian." During subsequent kickball games all the boys attempted (with, in some cases, surprising success) many of the hot dog maneuvers for which Randy had been famous. In the months that followed, the three weaker boys performed with greater competence than ever before. What had been embodied in Randy, a collectively shared grandiose self-representation for the other boys was, in a matter of weeks, mimicked, mourned and then transformed into a less grand but more solidly competent self-representation presented through their own performance.

Each boy's individual issues remained personally salient; as they made more or less progress, each at his own pace, this shift in collective self-representation marked a significant improvement in the self-esteem experienced by three of the remaining four boys in the group.

Discussion and Concluding Remarks

In concluding we'd like to return to the three questions raised at the beginning of this paper.

Is Peer Group Culture in Itself a Curative Factor in Children's Group Psychotherapy?

To a great extent this would appear to depend upon the particular problems with which a child enters treatment. If a child's ego is essentially intact, and conflict is not severe, but he or she is still having difficulty forming satisfactory peer relationships, it is possible that an inability to participate in indigenous peer culture is itself a significant problem in need of remediation. For such children participation in some form of group therapy may in fact provide a safe context to feel less isolated and develop greater self esteem.

Following Winnicott (1951, 1967) a psychotherapy group may be considered a holding environment within which a child is provided the opportunity to create transitional phenomena. For children with moderately impaired object relations, but otherwise intact egos, what we are calling "peer group culture" may function in part as transitional phenomena which, within the context of the group as holding environment, may help repair a child's damaged object relationed capacity.

For ego-impaired or severely conflicted children—who are also socially isolated—inclusion in peer culture can be important but is not in itself curative. For seriously impaired children, participation in peer culture within the context of a psychotherapy group may provide a fleeting glimpse of unity with the object (Winnicott 1967) or psychic organization, but can not itself foster a consistent capacity to organize the complexities of intrapsychic and psychosocial life. For such children perhaps the most significant curative factor is the extensive transferential relationships with the therapist and other children, which provide a context within which separation and individuation may be recapitulated and structure may slowly emerge. Only later in work with these children can they make sufficient use of peer culture for it to become an important therapeutic factor.

How Does Peer Culture Provide the Therapist with a Point of Access to the Representational and Psychosocial Worlds of His or Her Clients?

This point has been addressed throughout the clinical examples cited in this paper. For instance, we discussed how collective and individual self representations were revealed in the statue game and how a clear status hierarchy was revealed through kickball in one boys group. In another group recall how the "bad boys" masculine strivings and wishes for an organizing calm became apparent through their embracing peer culture in the video arcade. This leads to our final question.

When and How Can the Development of the Peer Group Culture Be Influenced by the Therapist with Reference to Particular Therapeutic Goals?

By definition, indigenous peer culture cannot be introduced by the therapist; the therapist can only structure the group so as to provide an arena within which elements of the indigenous peer culture can be introduced and expressed by the children, and can then be appealed to by the therapist in pursuit of particular therapeutic goals. Thus in one latency-aged boy's group, in a video arcade when one boy continuously jostled the arm of another, disrupting his game, the therapist only needed to say, "I've never seen that sort of thing happen in an arcade before," for the group to engage in intensive clarifying of rules consistent with indigenous peer culture. This highlights the importance of the space and materials available to the group, for they define the arena within which indigenous peer culture may or may not be expressed; for example, taking the "bad boy" group to the local pizzeria equipped with video games provided them with an opportunity to embrace the conventions of the arcade, as previously described.

There are also aspects of indigenous peer culture that are hurtful to certain children, such as the latency-aged peer group's natural propensity for scapegoating. Here the therapist—through verbalization, modeling, and limit setting—intervenes, and provides an alternative system of organizing self and object representations and regulating affect. When the therapist "stops the action" to clarify or interpret a conflict that has just occurred between two children; or says, "When people's feelings get hurt in this group, we talk about it," he or she is introducing values and meanings that may be quite alien to the peer culture, and at times even to the larger adult culture. This might be considered the point at which indigenous peer culture ends and therapeutic group culture begins. Indeed, we might think of children's inclusion of maladaptive aspects of indigenous peer culture in the psychotherapy group as an invitation to the therapist to show them a better way.

In summary, peer group culture functions as a significant variable in group psychotherapy with children. We have attempted to illustrate in this paper how an understanding of the significance of culture in organizing psychological phenomena may provide group therapists with greater access to the representational and psychosocial worlds of their clients. We have further attempted to illustrate how this access may provide the therapist(s) greater therapeutic leverage with the group as a whole as well as with individual children.

REFERENCES

Bion, W.R., *Experience in Groups*, London, Tavistock Publishers, 1961.
Erikson, E.H., *Childhood and Society*, New York, Norton & Co., 1963.
Erikson, E.H., *Identity and the Life Cycle*, New York, W. W. Norton & Co., 1980.
Frank, M., "Modifications of Activity Group Therapy: Responses to Ego Impoverished Children," *Clinical Social Work Journal*, V.4 (2), 1976.
Frank, M., "Personal Communication," 1983.
Freud, A., "Emotional and Social Development" in *The Writings of Anna Freud*, V.5, New York, International Universities Press, 1969.
Gabriel, B., "An Experiment in Group Treatment," *American Journal of Orthopsychiatry*, V.9 p.16-151, 1939.
Garland, J. and Frey, L., "Application of Stages of Group Development to Groups in Psy-

chiatric Settings" in Bernstein, S. (ed.) *Further Explorations in Group Work,* Charles River Books, Boston, Ma., 1965.

Garland, J., Jones, H. and Kolodny, R. "A Model for Stages of Development in Social Work Groups" in Bernstein, S. (ed.), *Exploration in Group Work: Essays in Theory and Practice,* Boston University School of Social Work, 1965, p.14.

Geertz, C., *Interpretations of Culture,* Basic Books, New York, 1975.

Ginnott, H., *Group Psychotherapy with Children,* New York, McGraw Hill, 1961.

Grunebaum, H. and Solomon L., "Toward A Peer Theory of Group Psychotherapy, I: On the Developmental Significance of Peers and Play," *International Journal of Group Psychotherapy,* 1980, 30; 23-49.

Grunebaum, H. and Solomon, L., "Toward A Theory of Peer Relationships II: On the Stages of Social Development and Their Relationship to Group Psychotherapy," *International Journal of Group Psychotherapy,* 1982, 32; 283-307.

Kaplan, E., "Manifestations of Aggression in Latency and Pre Adolescent Girls," *The Psychoanalytic Study of the Child,* V.31, p.63-69, New Haven: Yale University Press, 1975.

Kohut, H., *The Analysis of the Self,* International University Press, New York, 1971.

Kohut, H., *The Restoration of the Self,* International Universities Press, New York, 1971.

Le Vine, R.A., "The Psychoanalytic Study of Lives in Natural Social Settings," *Human Development,* 14;100-109, 1971.

Le Vine, R.A., *Culture, Behavior and Personality,* Aldine, Chicago, 1973.

Le Vine, S. and Pfeifer, G., "Separation and Individuation in an African Society: The Developmental Tasks of the Gusii Married Woman," *Psychiatry,* v. 45, pp. 61-75.

Mahler, M., Pine, F. and Bergman, A., *The Psychological Birth of the Human Infant,* Basic Books, New York, 1975.

Papell, C. and Rothman, B., "Relating the Mainstream Model of Social Work with Groups to Group Psychotherapy and the Structured Group Approach," *Social Work with Groups,* 3 (2): 5-23, 1980.

Pfeifer, G. and Weinstock-Savoy, D., "The Natural History of a Pre-Adolescent Boys Psychotherapy Group," Paper presented to the faculty of the Brookline Mental Health Center and the Brookline Public Schools, April 1982.

Sandler, J. and Rosenblatt, B., "The Concept of Representational World," *Psychoanalytic Study of the Child,* V. 17, pp. 128-145, 1962.

Schamess, G., "Group Treatment Modalities for Latency-Age Children," *International Journal of Group Psychotherapy* 26; 455-474, 1976.

Scheidlinger, S., "Activity Group Therapy with Primary Behavior Disorders in Children," *The Practice of Group Therapy,* ed. Slavson, New York, 1947.

Scheidlinger, S., "Three Group Approaches With Socially Deprived Latency-Age Children," *International Journal of Group Psychotherapy,* 15:434-445, 1965.

Scheidlinger, S., "Group Therapy for 'Latency-Aged Children': A Birds Eye View," *Journal of Clinical Child Psychology,* 6(1);40-43, 1977.

Schiffer, M., "Permissiveness Versus Sanction in Activity Group Therapy," *International Journal of Group Psychotherapy,* 2; 255-261, 1952.

Schiffer, M., *The Therapeutic Play Group,* Grune & Stratton, New York 1969.

Slavson, S.R., "Criteria for Selection and Rejection of Patients for Various Types of Group Psychotherapy," *International Journal of Group Psychotherapy,* 5; 3-30, 1955.

Slavson, S.R., *An Introduction to Group Therapy,* New York, International Universities Press, 1945.

Slavson, S.R., "A Bio-quantum Theory of the Ego and its Applications to Group Psychotherapy," *International Journal of Group Psychotherapy,* 9;5-30, 1959.

Slavson, S.R., *A Textbook in Analytic Group Psychotherapy,* New York, International Universities Press, 1964.

Slavson, S.R. and Schiffer, M., *Group Psychotherapies for Children,* International Universities Press, New York, 1975.

Sullivan, H.S., *The Interpersonal Theory of Psychiatry,* Norton, New York, 1953.

Wilson, G. and Ryland, G., *Social Group Work Practice: The Creative Use of the Social Process,* Connecticut, Practioner's Press, 1981.

Winnicott, D.W., "Transitional Objects and Transitional Phenomena," *Through Pediatrics to Psychoanalysis,* Basic Books, New York 1975.

Winnicott, D.W., "The Location of Cultural Experience," *International Journal of Psychoanalysis,* V. 48 (3) 1967.

Yalom, I.D., *The Theory and Practice of Group Psychotherapy,* New York, Basic Books, 1975.

Differential Assessment and Treatment of the School Age Child: Three Group Approaches

James A. Garland
Jeffrey West

This paper focuses on three developmental issues commonly observed in young school aged treatment groups: (1) completion of early separation-individuation tasks; (2) resolution of pre-school, interpersonal family relationships; and (3) adaptation to latency peer culture. On the basis of a differential assessment of these developmental parameters, three group treatment approaches are described. We propose that components such as group composition, worker characteristics and modus operandi, program content, level and focus of intervention, and interpersonal patterning, can be adapted to meet the respective needs represented by the three developmental levels.

The hypotheses developed here are the result of a number of years of observation and clinical practice, although this represents their initial formal exposure.

Although time and space do not permit detailed discussion of the various ways in which children are classified with respect to treatment needs and preferred intervention routes, a brief discussion and critique of some current classification attempts is in order, to put our system into perspective. The divisions are somewhat arbitrary and organized to suit the focus of this study. The children are viewed in relation to: (1) degree of disturbance; (2) social and situational status; (3) chronological age; and (4) developmental theme.

James A. Garland, ACSW, LICSW, is Professor and Chairperson of Group Work, Boston University School of Social Work, Boston, Massachusetts. Jeffrey West, MSW, LICSW, is Coordinator of Group Treatment, Child and Family Clinic, South Shore Mental Health Center, Quincy, Massachusetts.

© 1984 by The Haworth Press, Inc. All rights reserved.

57

Degree of Disturbance

In reviewing the distinctions, both dynamic and behavioral, made by practitioners and theoreticians, we note some differences in opinion as to the efficacy of group treatment of the most severely disturbed youngsters, those described as autistic and psychotic. Some indicate that the process, with its emphasis on structured reality activity and focus on adult to child interaction, is not truly therapy through the group, but treatment in a group setting. A similar question is raised about socialization and personal care "training" groups for mentally retarded and cognitively impaired children. In both cases the preference is for small groups, a recognition of the limited interpersonal capacity of the seriously impaired child. We note the historic and field-related difficulty and vacillation in the capacity and willingness of workers and agencies to deal with groups of severely impulsive and anti-social boys and girls. Social group work agencies have, in their more courageous and innovative periods, dealt with the problem by working on the street corners in the youths' own turf or have gritted their teeth and acceded to a pattern of relative permissiveness (and chaos) in their own facilities. At other times they have vacillated by introducing less personal, more highly regimented recreational programs and if those did not work, as they often did not with the most severely alienated and impulsive girls and boys, have excluded them, sadly concluding that they were "not able to use the program." Clinical agencies have often insulated themselves from the problem via selective intake processes wherein children of this type never really become clients. In other cases, well intended attempts to apply regressive and cathartic group modes have resulted in psychic and physical injury to all involved, destruction of equipment and environment and general disruption of the routines and therapeutic calm of the institution. Lately we observe a more eclectic return to clearly defined contracting, moderately structured, non-regressive activity and focus on individual and group autonomy and competency building (Frank, 1976; MacLennon, 1977). In the higher levels of pathology we note that intensive, regressive-recapitulative group approaches are seen as being effective. Children on these levels, even when socially isolated or inept, are assumed to possess the variety of basic strengths that make them able to respond to the *sturm und drang* of the opening up process and as well to the demands for moderate interpersonal awareness and conformity. From a labelling point of view, the designations here group around mild character disorder and neurosis (Slavson, 1964, pp. 181-193 and 145-153; 1955). The differential question is raised as to whether with such a boy or girl we favor "returning" the child to the mid-level of a family-business oriented group or whether we think that the egocentricity is in a major way unfinished primary separation. We may on the other hand conclude that there is no future for this child in either the boudoir or the nursery, and decide to challenge the youngster to deal with the demand of libidinal sublimation and control of self-centered behavior as offered in the peer model group.

Social and Situational Status

We include this category, most explicitly dealt with in the range of group intervention exemplified by traditional social group work, to stress that an ongoing situation in a child's life may be an important factor in determining the level which is his or her dominant concern in the group.

Some examples will serve to illustrate: Two black eight-year-old boys in a group with four whites, exhibit clannishness, bring food to meetings which they do not share with the others and stick close to the group worker. They seek his approval in all matters and describe the other boys as being "cheap" and "trying to start fights." In game playing they imagine giant snowmen smashing into their rock etship. This behavior is reminiscent of some children who are dealing with separation-individuation level concerns, replete with splitting, dependency, projection, polarization and non-human annihilation fantasies, although we know from other information that these two boys are essentially healthier than that. It is not particularly difficult to discern reactions and protective adaptation to prior (and anticipated) experiences with racism, including being stoned in a school bus. One might say, simple enough. The problem, on a practice level, is not so simple. Experience shows that powerful psychological sets of this type can be contagious and, in a newly formed group, may call forth not only the all-too-available racist proclivities in the white boys; they may also serve in the transactional result to lower the general thematic functioning of the group and jeopardize any already precarious individual adjustments.

It is not uncommon for family crises—distinguished from long established family pathology—dramatically to affect the child's psychological orientation and group behavior. We have in mind a nine-year-old girl, the oldest of three sisters and working successfully at establishing her individuality and peerhood in public school and in a mental health center "social skills" group. She reacted to her parents' separation (father left the home) by becoming moody and underachieving in school, and in the group leading a rebellion of the other girls against the co-workers. She was alternately attacking and seductive with the male worker and accusatory ("cheap refreshments") and clinging with the woman. In the process of the turmoil which she provoked, it was noted that she was able to focus all of the interpersonal action and the activity program around herself; her indigenous leader activity was seen as essentially egocentric and reflective of fallen self-esteem and injured narcissism. The drama suggests a regression to earlier family concerns. In the same vein, it has been noted that children who have experienced repeated family dislocation (e.g., serial foster placement) and those who are called upon through circumstances of family economic hardship to assume premature parental responsibilities, often vacillate in the levels at which they function. Writers and practitioners have not explicitly identified a typology of regressive steps occasioned by situational stress. It is our contention, however, that the behavioral sets that are induced may be usefully categorized within the three levels being explicated in this discussion.

In the Matter of Age

Major attention to group involvement, whether on the level of treatment or growth and education, (as in schools, community recreation, boy and girl scouts) has commenced with the entry of the child into elementary school. Slavson (1952), for example, recommends that age seven and above is appropriate for application of activity and activity-interview group therapy. It is his (and others') view that the child below that age is not sufficiently oriented toward peers to make effective use of the group process in the service of treatment. Similarly, most writers in the social group work field have seen the pre-school child as being too egocentric and parentally oriented to make adequate use of the social interest and problem solving processes that are involved in successful peer cohesion and entry into citizenship training. Pre-school group participation has been, with some variation, centered around the adult parent surrogate, emphasizing parallel play and stimulation of interest in sibling-peers with some expectation of beginning social conformity. There is some disagreement in the field as to the "natural" maturational readiness of the child for adaptation to social peer interaction on other than an imitative level. In the case of pre-school youngsters who manifest developmental delays or give evidence of unusual difficulty in separating from parents, there is efficacy in conducting concurrent mother support and child play groups. In some cases the mothers and children are brought together with multiple workers in a fluid collective situation wherein multiple interactive levels and combinations are possible, with emphasis on activity as well as discussion and with active modeling on the part of the workers. In regard to opinions about the correct balance between verbal and attention modes there is considerable debate, even vacillation, among practitioners and in the literature. If there is any consistent trend it is that there is a correlation between increasing age and increasing use of discussion and reflection. In the matter of gender composition in relation to age, the differences in practice seem to be a reflection of setting (and by implication group purpose and goal) and developmental social tradition. There is a preference in both social group work and classical therapy circles for unisexual grouping (Klein, 1972, p. 64; Slavson, 1964, pp. 218-222) particularly within the latency and young adolescent spectrum. This position is buttressed theoretically on the grounds that dealing with feelings about issues of gender identity, sexuality, and parents, is often better accomplished in the *absence* of figures who exemplify these relational states—especially persons of the opposite sex. There is slightly more variation in composition in the combining of pre-schoolers with occasional reference to the conventional wisdom of the "naturalness" of family-like heterogeneous gender grouping. In settings which represent normal growth and socialization functions one sees higher incidence of mixing the sexes, particularly where there is a value orientation strongly in favor of promoting role flexibility. The realization of this goal is complicated by the conservative tendency on the part of young people (and adults for that matter) to develop gender-linked role specialization, complementarity and even polarity when they are intermixed (Carlock and Martin, 1977). The authors have had some success making the best of both worlds, so to speak, in bringing together reasonably advanced boy and girl groups for periodic encounters and integrative experience. It was found that both in preparation for and post-reflection on the heterosexual contact, the experiencing of the non-present opposite gender happened with great intensity and heightened learning. In a similar vein, the vicarious interchange and differential "practice" that are afforded between the rarified, unisexual clinical group and the everyday, normal (school, residential, family, neighborhood) heterosexual experience appear to have great cumulative potential, especially where workers in both arenas are sensitive to their healthful exploitation. Interestingly, clinical practice, whatever its special rationale, appears to follow traditional social practice of pre-school and later adolescent sex mixing and latency and early adolescent segregation. There is a large element in child treatment of the promotion of traditional growth norms and functions.

Developmental Theme

A problem in this area is that in too many cases in the literature and in practice, insufficient attention is paid to the difference between chronological and psycho-social age, both in composing groups and in determining with any degree of specificity what current or residual developmental issue is to be addressed in the group. It is not uncommon, for example, for workers to be vague when they group seven to nine year old children, as to how far the various youngsters have progressed away from preoccupation with family issues as compared to being able to concentrate on the concrete tasks and practical politics of the latency period. Similarly, it is too often true that in planning worker assignment to groups of eleven or thirteen year olds, there is a curious lack of investigation into the possibility that some of the youngsters may have gone beyond the industry stage and are beginning to reopen the door to sexuality. This tentative and unstable awakening may result in some cases in volatile and unproductive emotional reactions when the youngsters are confronted with a group worker of the opposite sex. It is important for our purposes to emphasize not only aspects of the child's problems that are described in terms of psychodynamic stresses, cognitive insufficiencies and the like, but also to develop a perspective that lets us know how the girl or boy is using that personal equipment in the context of the interpersonal sphere. Moreover, we must develop a mental picture of the child in relation to "how far" he or she has come in this regard, to visualize the child symbolically in a series of interpersonal gestalts.* We start with primary caretaker,

---

*Grunebaum and Solomon have contributed significantly (1980, 1982) to understanding of development of peer relations as a framework for group intervention.

secondary adult and child—the "mother and other" constellation; secondly moving to the more highly differentiated triangles and quadrangles of the preschool family; and thence to the autonomous and sometimes enslaving peer gang, with parents and teacher as background players.

Differential Intervention: Three Models

Having considered some of the elements involved in planning for child group treatment, we turn to recommendations for three models of group work designed to accommodate to the respective treatment needs. They are represented in brief in order to emphasize the distinctions and differences among them rather than the commonalities and overlaps. We rely on the reader's familiarity with group work to fill in some of the missing details (e.g., the minutiae of structure in play patterns in the various groups). Similarly, it must be understood that universals such as group developmental stages, the use of support, respect for individual integrity, proscription of physical violence and the like, run across all the models and that the ways in which they appear and are managed will tend to vary from group to group. Secondly, while differences are highlighted, one must keep in mind that emphasis or focal tendency is implied, not mutual exclusivity. For example, again using play structure to illustrate, it is recommended that in the separation (Model I) group there will be encouraged a looser organization as regards game playing and activity planning; whereas on the peer level (Model III) group there is an expectation of more complex rule-oriented game playing and more detailed and possibly binding planning for future events. On the other hand, there is an expectation that the Model I group will gradually move toward complexity and that Model III will leave space for regressive spontaneity and free play. A further qualifying note is that the models appear in pure form; reality is always more eclectic than ideal type. Similarly, we have observed that some groups which have started off at the more primitive level progress, in the course of their existence, through subsequent stages.

Model I

The first model is focused around the resolution of unfinished issues of separation individuation. Its basic tasks are: (1) to enable the child to regulate the psychological distance between self and other (particularly the adult); (2) to allow for some gratification of needs for closeness and nurturance; (3) at the same time to allow the girl or boy to escape the enveloping parental presence; and (4) to do some practicing in the service of autonomy in the presence of the worker. The initial view of other members, in the eyes of the individual child, is as obstacles to his/her access to the adult. It is expected, however, that through the successive steps of interstimulation, commonality of activity interest, imitation, discovery of a common threat (namely the monster-worker) and defensive cohesion to guard against that threat, will come a beginning level of mutual identification and positively based social cooperation. The composition of this group, if the members' chronological ages are in the upper ranges of latency, is preferably unisexual. This has to do with the inexorable intrusion of sexual interest and the need for identity formation in the company of those who are most like oneself, namely the same gender. At the same time it must be emphasized in this context that the task in Model I is *not* gender identity formation, but *personhood* and the achievement of an autonomous ego. Partly for that reason it appears that with younger children, worker and member composition may be heterosexual, and may in fact have the advantage—if only a slight one—of providing mother-father surrogate images against whom may be practiced the pre-oedipal push-pull process of ambivalence management and movement from symbiosis to social reality.

It is recommended that the age range be within three years, with tighter limits being imposed in the case of younger latency children. This rule should apply to all the models. In the matter of group size, it seems that more primitive youngsters, as in this model, have limited capacity both cognitively and affectively to deal with large numbers; a rough limit might be six. At the same time, we must guard against our own countertransference tendencies—probably based on family fantasies, desires to rescue the fragile infant, or fear of being ravaged and consumed by too many biting, sucking little mouths, and the like—which lead us time and again to construct groups of three or four children and two workers. We are in the business of allowing early childhood practicing, not reifying the family. It is our observation that the degree of accessibility to the adult offered by such small numbers (and low child-adult ratios) is seductive, in that it suggests that one to one union can be achieved. This arrangement can be terrifying in terms of adult-child valence, destructive to creation of a viable peer system and in the end counterproductive to the development of differentiation and autonomy.

If group size is adequate, then there is a slight preference here for two workers, provided it is clearly understood that their inclusion is in the interests of the children being able to play out the polarities of attachment-separation, affection-hostility and the like. It should not be based (and this rule should hold true for all the models) on: lack of supervision or consultation; workers who fear children's needs or aggressiveness and require a peer crutch; a student who needs a group to write a paper; or inadequate physical facilities that necessitate compensatory monitoring. Added to these admonitions is the caution that dual adult presence can lead to the institutionalization of good parent and bad parent splitting if care is not exercised to keep the situation fluid and moving. We are not particularly concerned about worker gender. It appears in the first place that the traditional bias in social group work for same-sex worker was often based on custom or on a misdiagnosis; that since one was dealing with latency kids the issue must be sexual identity, where in fact on Level I the issue as we have said is individuation and personhood. Secondly, observation of children's use of workers in these groups indicates that they will construe the adults' identity in whichever direction their need dictates. It is commonly noted, for example, that in the instance of a male-male or female-female co-worker team, one of the partners is, however subtly, related to as mommy and the other as daddy. Moreover, is it our hypothesis that although in custom, and perhaps in myth, traits such as nurturance, tenderness, assertiveness, leadership and the like are sex-linked, the exclusivity is often more apparent than real; and in fact, human growth issues are more universal than and transcendent of gender. In regard to our present discussion, dimensions such as cuddling versus stepping out independently, passive feeding versus mutual pot-lucking, and assertion versus compliance, appear to be accessible to modelling and resolution by both male and female workers.

The implication in this model for worker characteristics is that he or she must be the kind of person who is comfortable with the dualities represented in the early struggle for differentiation, particularly with the readiness to be alternately idealized and despised, consumed and spit out, and clung to and escaped from.

Level of intervention and group process and program are implicit in what has been said above and flow from the group theme and goal. There is some latitude for fantasy production (monster dramas), moderate regression (process oriented crafts, being wheeled around in a freight dolly), parallel play (individual craft projects) and only moderate expectation for participation in group games or collective decision making, at least at the outset of the group experience. On the other hand expressive and cathartic elements must be moderated and to an extent delimited by ego supportive structure. There is acceptance of the group system being, for some time, adult-centered, although as indicated previously, the goal is that imitation and commonality of interest, especially around the management of parents, will serve as a basis for subsequent collective action and mutual identification.

Model II

The second model is focused around *recapitulation of the pre-school family and the resolution of sibling rivalry and oedipal competition.* It allows for the beginning of the transition from egocentric preoccupation to investigation of objective and social reality. It assumes that the youngster is no longer preoccupied with initial separation and individuation and is ready cognitively and affectively to encounter the interpersonal complexities of triangles, quadrangles, and sub-groups as the primary arena of restitution and growth. It is assumed that though the child-client may be troubled about family issues, he or she, nevertheless, has the capacity to differentiate self from other and other from other as well.

In the course of comprehending and mastering the cognitive and emotional strain of this more complex interpersonal patterning, the child is naturally called upon to juggle higher numbers of behavioral alternatives and is energized by a greater array of stimuli. One of these stimulating complexities is the increasing awareness of and response to gender and sexuality. We have already raised a question as to whether the presence in a group of a person who is or who represents the object of crucial, emotional significance, is desirable in order for the matter in question to be worked through (note Slavson's [1964, pp. 138-140] caution about the dangers of "reality saturation" in psychotherapy groups). It appears from our practice and from research studies that more work on sexuality and feelings about the other gender takes place in the *absence,* as far as *members* are concerned, of that gender. For all these reasons we favor, in Model II groups, unisexual grouping.* Conversely there appears to

---

*A major exception to this guideline would be the case of children who have lost, through death or family dissolution, a sibling of the opposite sex. In these situations there appears to be a supportive and restitutional benefit in including both boys and girls.

be some value in having a worker of the opposite sex from the members. He or she seems to be more "usable" by the group in allowing them to express more openly, erotic, possessive and rivalrous feelings (i.e., as compared to other members). In this case it is preferable that the worker in question be a partner of a male-female team; thus allowing for a degree of safe testing of the oedipal paradigm while leaving somewhat more tranquil the bonds among the sibling members.

On the member to member level, it is important to recognize that the egocentricity, rivalry and vying for popularity and influence that the children exhibit is not solely or even in many cases principally, a displacement from feelings toward the adult(s). The "me first" orientation of the play age child (or one who is fixated at that level) can have a social reality that is functionally autonomous from child-adult concerns, although each sphere tends to infuse and modify the other. In the interventive context, it is important for the worker to try to differentiate the two. By way of illustration: the failure on the part of a girl to join in a group game and her decision instead to hang on the periphery near the male worker might, on careful examination, prove to be motivated by a primary desire to be close to him, to be his "favorite"; or it might be her reaction against the rule-oriented cooperative norm which would limit her desire for fantasy-fulfilling, individual make-believe play. His options might include involving his female partner to diffuse the attachment, playing and exploring with the girl, handing her a scorecard or doing nothing, depending on his assessment.

The vignette serves as well to indicate that in this group model the range for individualistic vs. collective organization and regressive vs. sublimated activity, may be quite broad.

Similarly, the role of the workers may be quite varied in terms of passive observer to active participant and *tabula rasa* to behavior modeler and mediator. The worker(s) should be sensitive to countertransference vulnerabilities in the areas of sexual narcissism, being in the various corners of the romantic triangle, sibling rivalry and individualism. They should be stable and flexible with respect to gender identity and role. The latter is typically encountered when children characterize workers in terms of traditional mommy-daddy role ascriptions that may be incompatible with the ways in which contemporary adults are trying to orient their lives.

Program activity follows family themes and has flexible parameters. It is possible to include in the physical armamentarium, materials ranging from dollhouse to baseball field and finger paint to plastic model. Play themes may range from Cinderella to Simon Says, organization from lap-sitting and solitary play to relay races, and verbal intervention from discussion of there-and-then family emotions to clarification of here-and-now social consequences.

Model III

As has been indicated previously, the peer, social group model most resembles the natural clubs formed by young school age children, with their emphasis on *transition away from the family.* Now is the time for learning the rules of social reality and conformity, developing cognitive skills having to do with classification, conservation and social morality (albeit an absolute brand), and employing all of these along with task oriented pragmatism, to put away the overtly sexual and egocentric preoccupation of pre-school years. The therapeutic adaptation of the natural form allows for expression of both the joyful creativity and the concomitant nastiness of the period. It attempts to modify, moderate and make conscious such phenomena as rigid and exclusionary classifications of gender, race, age, class and personal style at the same time that it aids in identity formation. It attempts to create a less demanding and arbitrary standard for progress and achievement at the same time that it focuses on teaching concrete and symbolic skills. It allows for moderate reversion to (or staying with) dependent and adult-oriented relational and activity states at the same time that it actively promotes individual autonomy and peer group identification and loyalty. And it seeks to keep alive healthy narcissism and to encourage questioning about all phenomena, from why adults make you do homework to the mysteries of masturbation, even as it models and teaches citizenship and sublimation.

Given the emphasis in intensive treatment groups on identity consolidation, the need for sublimation of libidinal impulses and the drive toward cognitive consistency (as a precursor to relativism), there is a clear preference for simplifying the cast of personal images; group membership should be unisexual. In this model, that unisexual composition extends to the worker as well, where the realities of staffing permit. Simplification applies also to numbers of workers. Even in the case of relatively impulsive groups, long term observation suggests that there is as good or even better potential for control with one worker as there is with two or three. Moreover, it is our contention that there is greater potential for reasonable balancing of power and autonomy between group and worker and a stronger inducement for members to turn to the group as a source of gratification and growth, with a single adult presence.

All of the foregoing points to the suggestion that the worker must be comfortable with a new level of symbiosis versus separation, namely that of vacillation between idealization and rebellion. Similarly this adult must relearn tolerance for and appreciation of the transitional utility of the child group's crude and arbitrary morality. She or he must be prepared to be an almost invisible bystander at one moment and mediator, arbitrator and debate coach at the next. The worker will be cathected as barely-disguised heterosexual and/or homosexual love object at one session and lawgiver at the next. The variable way in which the worker is perceived and utilized by the group, offers numerous opportunities for modeling and teaching of attitudes and skills consonant with development of psychologically free and non-bigoted citizens.

Conclusion

We have attempted to outline three approaches to group treatment of troubled children based on differential assessment of their psychosocial level of interpersonal development. Particular emphasis has been placed on distinguishing the respective basic themes and goals, member composition, worker characteristics, mode and level of intervention and implications for content and process of group operation and program. Application of the approaches presented here must be done eclectically, respecting the particular mix of variables present in any real practice situation. Caution and judgment must be exercised in accepting both the diagnostic premises of the study and the practical prescriptions that flow from them.

REFERENCES

Carlock, C.J. & Martin, P.Y. "Sex Composition and the Intensive Group Experience." *Social Work*, 1977, 22(1), 27-32.

Frank, M.G. "Modifications of Activity Group Therapy: Responses to Ego Impoverished Children." *Clinical Social Work Journal*, 1976, 4(2).

Grunebaum, H. & Solomon, L. "Toward a Peer Theory of Group Psychotherapy, I." *International Journal of Group Psychotherapy*, 1980, 30(1), 23-49.

Grunebaum, H. & Solomon, L. "Toward a Theory of Peer Relationship, II: On the Stages of Social Development and Their Relationship to Group Psychotherapy." *International Journal of Group Psychotherapy*, 1982, 32(4), 283-307.

Klein, A.F. *Effective Group Work.* New York: Association Press, 1972.

MacLennan, B.W. "Modifications of Activity Group Therapy for Children." *International Journal of Group Psychotherapy,* 1977, 27(1), 85-95.

Mahler, M., Pine, F. & Bergman, A. *The Psychological Birth of the Human Infant.* New York: Basic Books, Inc., 1975.

Slavson, S.R. *Child Psychotherapy.* New York: Columbia University Press, 1952.

Slavson, S.R. "Criteria for Selection and Rejection of Patients for Various Types of Group Psychotherapy." *International Journal of Group Psychotherapy,* 1955, 5(1), 3-30.

Slavson, S.R. *A Textbook in Analytic Group Psychotherapy.* New York: International Universities Press, Inc., 1964.

Resistance and Work in Adolescent Groups

Dermot J. Hurley

ABSTRACT. This paper examines the nature and function of resistance in adolescent groups and suggests that resistance can be better understood in the context of (a) stages of group development, and (b) work/resistance cycles which are the central mechanism of tension regulation in the group.

In contrast to adult groups, adolescent groups are blatant and direct in the types of resistances they employ to avoid the exploration of inner conflict and interpersonal tension. These resistances, used initially by the adolescent to maintain a sense of inner harmony, become the main avenue of tension regulation among group members. Defensive techniques* employed by adolescents include the "testing operations" and "diversionary tactics" described by MacLennan and Felsenfeld (1968, pp. 86-102) as well as the "group psychological expressions" of resistance described by Redl (1966, pp. 214-223). The former include operations such as complaining, blaming, attacking the leader, provoking, scapegoating, lateness, absenteeism, competitiveness, while the latter, described by Redl, includes such group resistances as escape into love, escape into virtue, protective provocation, and role confusion. Collusive resistance involving two or more members includes such activities as monopolizing, avoidance, silence, horseplay, and physical activi-

---

Dermont J. Hurley, MSW, is with Child & Family Centre, 58 Colborne Street, London, Ontario N6B 2R7.

*The terms "resistance" and "defense" are used interchangeably. According to Greenson, Freud used the terms synonymously throughout most of his writings. Here, the terms refer to any behaviour that the adolescent uses to avoid change. It is behaviour that hinders the work of therapy and maintains the status quo. For an indepth psychoanalytic study of the topic, see Chapter 2, "Resistance," in *The Technique and Practice of Psychoanalysis,* Vol.1., Ralph R. Greenson, London, The Hogarth Press, 1978.

71

ty (MacLennan & Felsenfeld, 1968). "Shared Rebelliousness" (Meeks, 1980), is frequently noted in adolescent groups and describes much the same process outlined by the other writers. To a greater or lesser extent, these defensive techniques are to be found in all adolescent groups. The frequency and predictability of these occurrences leads one to believe that these actions are not merely random, individualized, defensive manoeuvers but are in fact, highly structured interactions that are crucial to the development of the group. The quality and frequency of these resistances is aptly described by the term "organized chaos" which might have been coined to describe the complex interweaving of resistance and work that is so typical of adolescent groups.

The relationship between acting out (i.e., creating disturbances) and tension reduction in adolescents is well known (Blos, 1979; p. 254) and as early as 1925 Aichorn noted that aggressive behaviour in delinquent boys increased following periods of deep emotional expression and closeness. The relationship between acting out and affectionate feelings in adolescents is further confirmed by Offer, Marohn, Ostrov (1975, 32, pp. 1180-1186).

Despite the fact that group resistance has very often been described as the group expression of an individual's resistance, the notion of a shared psychological or emotional state underlies these formulations. In the work of Bion (1959), Ezriel (1957), shared unconscious states is the fundamental concept in analytic group work and they have offered elaborate psychoanalytic formulations of resistance and work in group that have done much to explain the enigma of group resistance to change. Patterns of work and disruption have been described by many adolescent group workers, particularly those in residential or milieu therapy centres. Though this paper describes typical patterns found in outpatient therapy groups, Crabtree and Levinson's (1980) work on the management of oscillatory cycles of tension in an adolescent therapeutic community comes closest to describing the work/resistance cycles outlined in this paper. Oscillatory cycles of tension "arise from fluctuations in relationship patterns among patients and staff leading to cycles of tension interaction in the group" (Crabtree & Levinson, 1980, pp. 512-589). These authors describe phases of rising tension, sometimes seasonal, in which deviancy erupts, often in the form of collective disturbance following a tension peak which is then followed by an abatement of tension and a period of "renewal and reconstruction" (Crabtree & Levinson, 1980). They credit much of their work to the pioneering work of such authors as Stanton and

Schwartz (1959) and Rapoport (1960). Slavson (1964) also describes a similar cycle of "equilibrium/disequilibrium" which he called "nodal and antinodal group behaviour" and noted that "conflicts, fights, playful hilarity, and destructiveness are regularly followed by periods of quiet and more or less constructive activity" (Slavson, 1964, pp. 46-49). He suggests that group contagion is the main force underlying these processes and considers the reduction in cyclical behaviour an indication of the group's maturity as well as a "barometer of internal changes in the patient" (Slavson, 1964, p. 48).

Helpful as these contributions are toward articulating a theory of resistance in adolescent groups, they do not explain the "mechanics" of group resistance, or the part resistance plays in the overall development of the group process.

In attempting to differentiate between the various forms of resistance found in adolescent groups, the author has found it helpful to group these into certain fairly well established resistance behaviours that are typical for various stages in the development of the group and are found to be more or less consistent from group to group. These are:

1. Resistances in the service of defining group structure.
2. Resistances employed to regulate group tensions.
3. Resistances used to deal with separation and termination.

Resistances in the Service of Defining Group Structure

These are techniques employed in the pre-affiliation group to test limits, provoke a leadership response and to define issues of distance/closeness, trust/mistrust, control, safety, etc. Typically, the adolescent tests the limits and forces the group worker to define the structures. Resistant behaviours include task avoidance, laughing or giggling, distracting, boasting, threatening, etc. and a variety of testing operations outlined by MacLennan and Felsenfeld (1968). Once the dominant pattern of interpersonal relationships is established and some degree of cohesiveness achieved, the stage is set for real therapeutic work to begin. Adolescents characteristically either barely "wet their toes" or "jump in with both feet." For some adolescents, inability to tolerate anxiety forces them into premature "confessions" which cause panic among other group members. Others may isolate and tune out in the face of mounting group tensions. At this stage in the life of the group, the group workers will have modelled a form of interpersonal dialogue which may be very threatening, as may be the stated task of the group which has been repeated many times, i.e., to share problems and feelings and work together on these. Though adolescent groups vary greatly in their cultures of openness versus closedness, sharing versus withholding, etc., each group seems to evolve over time a characteristic mode of tension regulation or a system of checks and balances which becomes an integral part of the overall interactional structure of the group. Without some mechanism of tension regulation, no group would survive for long and would be in danger of either gross overstimulation or total interactional paralysis—leading ultimately to complete fragmentation of the group.

Resistances Employed to Regulate Group Tensions

The Work/Resistance Cycle. These are techniques for regulating group tensions during the work phase. By now (2-4 months, depending on the group) the structure is known, dependable and predictable and the members have some guarantee of empathic resonance with the group leaders. This is the period of work/resistance cycles which continues throughout the life of the group varying only in intensity and duration from one phase to another. The central mechanism of tension regulation in adolescent groups is the work/resistant cycle. It is a function of the total group behaviour and involves the participation whether active or passive, conscious or unconscious of all the members. Work and resistance are viewed as two forms of group energy that are constantly at work in the group in a cyclical fashion to maintain group tension within acceptable limits, and allow for certain content, particularly affective communications to proceed within a certain definite range. If, during the work period, the optimum range is exceeded, then counter-work forces are activated to ease tension and recalibrate the range. Frequently in adolescent groups, as one member assumes a work posture, another adopts a counter-work position or signals their readiness for disruptive or distracting behaviour.

Two case illustrations outline how this works.

Example 1

The group. An outpatient young adolescent mixed group in their seventh (7th) month of weekly meetings, is comprised of 5 girls and 4 boys. An emerging theme for many weeks has been their profound disappointment with fathers and a corresponding exaggerated reliance on idealized mothers.

> *Alex* (picking up on Richard's theme of how hard it is to get along with mom's boyfriend): "We're taking dad to Court—the jerk won't pay anything."
>
> *Rob:* "He has to. . .they'll garnishee his wages."
>
> *Alex:* "He still won't pay (with feeling). . .my mother's working so hard just to keep things going."
>
> *Jim* (to Sue, with feigned hurt): "Stop smirking at me. . . you're making me laugh."
>
> *Sue:* "No I'm not! You're looking at me." (Both laughing boisterously.)
>
> *Alex* (continues unperturbed): "I just don't know what mom's going to do. (angrily) My father is such an asshole."
>
> *Lila* (to Sue and Jim): "Do you guys mind? Will you shut up the two of you. You're always behaving like little kids."
>
> *Jennifer* (turns to Mary and starts to whisper and giggle): "This has nothing to do with the group."

Alex continues—seemingly unperturbed by the disturbances. The group now seems to be totally uninvolved with Alex's problems.

> *Group Worker* (interjects): "The group seems to be having a hard time tonight listening to what Alex has to say about his dad. Maybe it's too hurtful to talk about how disappointing parents can sometimes be?"

Later, a rich discussion emerges in which:

A. Rob elaborated in depth on his anger towards his mother for forcing a new "father" on him.
B. Sue spoke of her father's "removal" from the family for a prolonged psychiatric illness.
C. Lila (in the following group) for the first time openly acknowledged that she had been victimized sexually by her stepfather.
D. Jim (in subsequent sessions) revealed his fears and anxiety

about his parents' violence and his removal into care for two
years when he was younger.

Ironically, when members signal discomfort in a particular area
and set themselves in opposition to the working group, then work
can proceed. The assumption is that the collective resistance of the
members is safely contained in one member and can rapidly be activated whenever tension regulation is required. In adolescent
groups, the member most sensitive or vulnerable in a particular area
(or simply the one least able to handle an issue on a particular day)
acts as a reassurance to the other members so that they may engage
safely in the work group.

Example II

Same group as Example 1.
Margaret's psychosomatic complaints and hysterical reactions to
blood, bodily processes, or gory stories, gave her "permission" to
walk out of the group any time she chose, dramatically disturbing
the group process when she did so. Very often one or other group
member "activated" her. . .this resistant ploy served *both* her narcissistic needs and the group's need for tension regulation.

> *Claire* (A provocative, "sexually sophisticated," 16 year-old,
> talking about sex and violence in a 'biker's' group known to
> her): "Those guys do anything they want with you. . .they
> don't hurt you though, unless there's a good reason (starts to
> recount some vivid stories of what happened to some friend of
> hers).

The group edges close to dealing with some real issues to do with
sexuality.

> *Jim* (to Margaret): "Jeez, you look awful pale. (to the
> group). . .I bet she's going to be sick!"
>
> *Margaret:* "I'll throw up in a minute for sure."
>
> *Claire* (continues): "So why is it only guys that can screw
> around; why should they have all the fun?"

A heated argument ensues among the group members. Margaret
exits, pale and sickly.

Jim: "What did we do now?"

Sue: "I know she doesn't like fighting or arguing. She hears a lot of bitching at home."

If tension runs high and the disruptive behaviour of one individual is "insufficient" or inappropriately challenged by the group leaders, then another member will engage with the first to help strengthen the resistance posture of the first member. Tension regulation is then achieved and the work resistance cycle maintained.

Resistances Used to Deal with Separation and Termination

The final stage in the group process may bring with it a reoccurrence of earlier forms of resistance and generally more regressive types of behaviour. A variety of techniques are used to prolong the group and avoid dealing with separation as the group moves towards closure. Fantasies of "fusion" and "togetherness" are common and the group behaves as if it is just another transition point in the life of the group. A particularly skillful ploy is the exclusion of the group leaders from the discussion. To some extent, the group members behave as if they had been already abandoned. Being taken care of is a major theme that often emerges in symbolic ways, and in one termination group, the group's dependency needs were displaced onto a hamster that was brought into the final session by an adolescent. The separation process is, of course, greatly compounded by the worker's own unacknowledged ambivalence about separation. Resistances include lateness, absenteeism, exaggerated problems, helplessness, subgrouping, extra group activities, excessive pairing, devaluing the leaders, splitting, denial, and generally, an overall increase in acting out both inside and outside the group. Some attempts are made to replicate the parent group elsewhere. Often the adolescents themselves are "just leaving for the summer" and expect to begin again in the fall.

Implications for Treatment

Since resistance is endemic to adolescent groups it is possible to plan interventions that maximise the likelihood of work and resistance occurring simultaneously at various points in the life of the group.

Planned interventions (i.e., strategic interventions) are more likely to work if the following points are kept in mind.

1. Adolescents do not resist change, they resist being changed (Vorrath and Brendtro, 1974).
2. Group allows the adolescent the possibility of defying and surrendering without contradiction (Buxbaum, 1945).

It is important that the group worker adopt a posture that he/she is not asking individuals to change but expects the group to change. There is always a clear unequivocal expectation that change will occur. The paradox of being told to stay as you are (individually) while being expected to change (collectively) mirrors the contradictory nature of adolescent relationships. (The adolescent in defying the parents' attempt to change his/her behaviour, enters a group which in reality exerts a much greater influence on his/her growth and development.) In a group an adolescent can change and resist change without contradiction.

The following is a brief summary of the techniques found most useful in promoting work in adolescent groups. Though employed elsewhere (Frankl, 1960), (Erickson, 1975), (Rabkin, 1977) notably with individuals and families (Haley, 1963, 1976), (Selvini Palazzoli, 1978) and the Palo Alto MRI group (1974, 1978), these strategies can be usefully adopted to group situations (Goldberg, 1980, pp. 287-297). Here, however, their use is employed with minimally diadic relationships only when the target behaviour relates to the total group behaviour.

All these techniques have in common the acceptance of resistance, and resistant behaviour is continually redefined as the members' contribution to the development of the group. Ironically resistance promotes cohesiveness which is the foundation of all group work.

Some strategies are used singly while others are used in combination (e.g., restraint and prescribing). The following list is not thought to be exhaustive.

1. Positive connotation
2. Restraining
3. Prescribing
4. Reframing
5. Seeding Ideas

Positive Connotation

Throughout the life of the group the group worker positively connotates behaviours (resistance) between members that are in the service of the groups developmental needs.

For example:

"All this bickering helps the group sort out how conflict should be handled in the group." Used in conjunction with other strategies (e.g., prescribing) positive connotation can have a powerful impact on group members. Positive connotation of resistance can be compared to a similar process in family therapy where the therapist positively connotates the "homeostatic tendency" (Palazzolli, 1978, Ch. 7) which is thought to be essential to the survival of the family. Acceptance of resistance with positive connotation can have much the same effect on the group as its counterpart has with families. The net result is often to provide the momentum necessary for the system (group) to transform itself.

Restraining

Early in the life of the group, co-workers model a form of communication that they hope the group will adopt. However the group are discouraged from "rushing in and spilling their feelings." They are told that it takes time to get to know each other. This reassurance often has the effect of promoting risk taking and sharing.

Prescribing

Prescribing is used to facilitate group development by asking the members to continue what they are already doing.

For example, group members might be asked to continue boisterous or play acting behaviour as it provides an outlet for the entire group emotion.

Reframing

Reframing is consistently used and specific resistant behaviours are given a positive connotation.

For example, monopolizing is called "allowing one person to do all the work on behalf of the group."

Seeding Ideas

Where the group seem to be avoiding a particular issue the group worker might take the position that it is "much too early to have a serious discussion about sex," adding that "it will probably take place sooner or later anyway."

Regardless of which strategies are used it is important that all interpretations be tentative and systemic i.e. they must account for the *total behaviour* of the group within the context (i.e., developmental phase), in which it occurs. Resistance is never negatively interpreted or challenged directly.

Summary

This paper has outlined how resistance is used in adolescent groups to regulate tension within the group. Resistance is viewed as being in the service of the group's "developmental needs," despite its obvious defensive purposes. In addition to the normal resistance encountered in group, there is in the life of any group, the recurring week to week avoidance of getting down to work and becoming task oriented. An oppositional mood is often present at the beginning of each group and is brought about simply by the "daily residue" of feelings, either about home or school which are often urgent and immediate for the adolescent. In addition, it is worth noting the characterological defensiveness that is present in anyone in a social situation where they may at any moment be called upon for an interpersonal contribution or commitment to an ongoing group process. The main implication for practice is that group workers must be able to identify and work with these resistances and help promote and shape behaviours that are in the interest of the group's needs. A sensitive and strategic approach to resistance is required rather than a purely interpretative or confrontative approach that may lead to further resistance and hinder the work of the group.

REFERENCES

Aichorn, A. 1925. *Wayward Youth,* 1960, Meridian Books, New York.
Berkowitz, I. (Ed.) *Adolescents Grow in Groups: Experiences in Adolescent Group Psychotherapy,* 1972, Brunner/Mazel, New York.
Bion, W.R. *Experiences in Groups.* London, Tavistock Publications, 1961.
Blos, P. *The Adolescent Passage,* 1979, International Universities Press Inc., New York.
Buxbaum, E. Transference and Group Formation in Children and Adolescents. *Psychoanalytic study of the child,* 1945, 1, 351-356.

Crabtree, L.H., Jr., and Levinson, D.F. Recurrent large-group phenomena: studies of an adolescent therapeutic community in *Adolescent Psychiatry Developmental and Clinical Studies,* VOL. VIII, Feinstein, Giovacchini, Looney, Schwartzberg and Sorosky (Eds.)., The University of Chicago Press, 1980, pp. 512-529.

Erickson, M., and Rossi, E., Varieties of double bind. *American Journal of Clinical Hypnosis,* 1975, 17, 143-157.

Ezriel, H. The Role of Transference in Psycho-Analytical and Other Approaches to Group Treatment. *Acta. Psychother.* (suppl.), 1957, pp. 101-116.

Frankl, V. Paradoxical Intention. A Logotherapeutic Technique. *American Journal of Psychotherapy,* 14, pp. 520-535.

Goldberg, C. The utilization and limitations of paradoxical intervention in group psychotherapy. *International Journal of Group Psychotherapy,* 1980, 3, VOL XXX.

Haley, J. *Strategies of Psychotherapy,* 1963, Grune and Stratton, New York.

Haley, J. *Problem—Solving Therapy,* 1976, Jossey-Bass, San Francisco.

Kraft, I.A. An Overview of Group Therapy with Adolescents. *International Journal of Group Psychotherapy,* 1968, 18, 461.

Levine, B. Reflections on Group Psychotherapy with Adolescents with some Implications for Residential Treatment in *Social Work with Groups,* Vol. 2, 1978.

MacLennon, B.W., and Felsenfeld, N. *Group Counseling and Psychotherapy with Adolescents,* 1968, Columbia University Press, New York & London.

Marshall, R.J. The treatment of resistances in psychotherapy of children and adolescents. *Psychotherapy Theory Res. Pract.,* 9 (2), 1972, 143-148.

Meeks, J.E. Adolescent Development and Group Cohesion. In *Adolescent Psychiatry Developmental and Clinical Studies,* Feinstein and Giovacchini (Eds.), 1980, The University of Chicago Press, Chicago.

Offer, D., Marohn, R.C., and Ostrov, E., *Violence Among Hospitalized Delinquents, Archives of General Psychiatry,* 1975, 32, 1180-1186.

Redl, F. *When we deal with children.* Selected writings, 1966, The Free Press, New York. pp. 214-223.

Rosenthal, L. Some dynamics of resistance and therapeutic management in adolescent group therapy. *Psychoanalytic Rev,* 1971, 58, 353.

Schwartz, W., and Zalba, S.R., *The Practice of Group Work,* 1971, New York, Columbia University Press.

Selvini Palazzoli, M., Cecchin, G.F., Prata, G., and Boscolo, L.S. *Paradox and Counter Paradox,* 1978, Jason Aronson, New York.

Slavson, S.R., and Schiffer, M. *Group Psychotherapies for Children. A Textbook,* 1975, International Universities Press, Inc.

Sugar, M. (Ed.) *The Adolescent in Group and Family Therapy,* 1975, Brunner/Mazel, New York.

Vorrath, H., and Brendtro, L.V. *Positive Peer Culture,* 1974, Aldine Publishing Company, Chicago.

Watzlawick, P., Weakland, J., and Fisch, R. *Change: Principles of Problem Formation and Problem Resolution,* 1974, Norton, New York.

Watzlawick, P. *The Language of Change,* 1978, Basic Books, New York.

Weakland, J., Fisch, R., Watzlawick, P., and Budin, H., Brief Therapy: Focused Problem Resolution. *Family Process,* 1974, 13:141-168.

CALL FOR PAPERS

in conjunction with

THE CENTENNIAL CELEBRATION

of the

LIFE AND WORKS OF
BERTHA CAPEN REYNOLDS
1885-1978

PROGRAMS: AMERICAN ORTHOPSYCHIATRIC ASSOCIATION ANNUAL MEETING
New York City—Monday, April 22, 1985

SMITH COLLEGE SCHOOL FOR SOCIAL WORK
Northampton, MA—Weekend June 28-30, 1985

AWARDS: Up to six papers will be chosen to receive the Frank C. Bancroft Award ($500). Selected papers may be published.

CATEGORIES: Manuscripts from faculty, students and practitioners will be judged separately.

CRITERIA: Papers may deal with any aspect of Bertha C. Reynolds work and writing—her philosophy, teaching practice, relation to the labor movement, contributions to social policy, minority and women's issues, social work theory and social action. Examination of both the historical and contemporary relevance of Reynold's contributions is involved. Manuscripts will be judged on the basis of scholarship, creativity, contributions to the field and relevance to centennial purpose.

FORMAT: Manuscripts of up to 20 double spaced typewritten pages may be submitted (4 copies). Use of style guide recommended—Publication Manual of the American Psychological Association, 2nd edition, 1974.

DEADLINE: December 1, 1984. Submit manuscripts to *Dr. Catherine Riessman, Smith College School of Social Work, Northampton, MA 01063.* Selections announced March 16, 1985.

SELECTION COMMITTEE: Dr. George Getzel, Hunter College School of Social Work, Dr. Shirley Jenkins, Columbia University School of Social Work, Prof. Barbara Joseph, Hofstra University, Labor Studies Program, Dr. Catherine Riessman, Smith College School of Social Work.

Groupwork with Abused Adolescent Girls: A Special Challenge

Julianne Wayne
Karen K. Weeks

ABSTRACT. Youthful victims of abuse and neglect can be helped to cope with their situations through group treatment. Their often provocative behavior, however, makes them especially difficult to work with. The following paper focuses on both therapeutic techniques with this population and ways to help the workers deal with the personal stress created by working with acting-out group members.

There is an irony in attempting groupwork practice with the youthful victims of abuse and neglect. The very characteristics which indicate there are benefits to be gained through group treatment also make groupwork with them a most difficult challenge. As their parents did decades earlier, such children, with their patterns of poor peer relationships and distrust of others, have already been successful at avoiding closeness with people who could help them cope with the terrible stresses they experience in their daily lives. It is imperative that this movement towards social isolation be reversed if the inter-generational cycle of abuse and neglect is to be stopped.

Julianne Wayne, EdD, is Acting Associate Dean, Boston University School of Social Work. Karen K. Weeks, MSW, is Clinical Social Worker, Catholic Charities Center of Old Colony, Area, Brockton, MA.

The authors wish to thank Joan Kenney, co-leader of the group for four years, for her special contribution to the development of this paper, and to acknowledge Betty Morningstar and Carolyn Poldvian for their initiative and skill in getting the group started.

83

This paper will describe and analyze a five year long groupwork experience with abused and neglected girls who were eight and nine years old when the group was first organized and who are thirteen and fourteen years old as of this writing. It is written from the dual perspectives of one of the group's two co-workers and of the group-work consultant who worked with them both. This paper will include an examination of the effect of the experience on the professionals as well as on the members. The argument will be made that professionals engaged in this work must be provided support from within their agency in order to sustain the energy and motivation level demanded to successfully meet the challenge such a group provides.

Before going further, it is important to emphasize that this will not be a story with an "all lived happily ever after" ending. At age fourteen, the story of these girls' lives is hardly "ended". What may be their most turbulent years still lie ahead. Indeed, almost each encounter with them reveals new areas of concern. However, there have been successes over the years, and it is important to recognize and savor these and to offer them as encouragement to others who would consider working with a similar group.

The Abused Child

Several studies identify the special characteristics of abused children.

Kinard cites research findings which indicate that abused children have particular problems with respect to aggression, self-concept, relationships with peers and adults, and the capacity to trust others. He goes on to point to the dearth of social services offered directly to them by indicating that most mental health intervention is directed towards the abusing parents.

> Attention to the child has been confined mainly to providing medical care for physical injuries and to ensuring protection from further physical harm. . .Recent studies. . .indicate that these children have serious emotional problems despite the services provided to their families.[1]

In their discussion of sexually abused children, Knittle and Tuana refer to their (1) feelings of isolation and alienation from peers, (2) distrust of adults and authority figures, (3) fear of closeness with therapists and (4) below average development of basic social skills.[2] They assert that group therapy is a more effective treatment modality in dealing with these characteristics than are individual or family therapies.

Timm concludes from her study of children remaining in the homes of their sociopathic parents (as often is the case with abused children) that they suffered from impaired cognitive and moral functioning. Fortunately, her study also reveals that these deficits can be overcome with appropriate intervention. She states that:

> group homes may provide a safer and more caring environment than sociopathic parents are able to give. . .A setting that provides more participation in decision-making, more role-taking opportunities and encourages group identity on the part of the children offers new hope.[3]

A Groupwork Service Begins

In recognition of these youngsters' special needs, two social workers at the Catholic Charitable Bureau of Brockton, Massachusetts took initiative in developing a groupwork service for their abused young clients. They believed that such a group would provide the context within which to terminate the cross-generational cycle of child abuse and neglect. The first step towards this would be to help the girls successfully deal with the normal developmental tasks of pre-adolescence made more complicated by their histories of neglect and physical and sexual abuse. The group was designed to include both discussion and activity.

Referrals to the group came from the agency's own protective service program, as well as from the Department of Social Service and schools in the area. After some shifts in membership, the group stabilized to the same seven members for most of its five years. Each family had an assigned caseworker to follow through with appropriate services as needed; e.g., when episodes of serious abuse developed.

The girls knew that the agency was involved with their families because of neglectful and/or abusive parenting and the group was presented to them as a vehicle for finding ways to deal with the difficulties of their situations. The activities were offered as a means to becoming better acquainted and enjoying their time together.

Subsequent to the initial ten week pilot project, group meetings were scheduled to coincide with the school calendar, beginning in September and ending in June with two all-day outings during the intervening summers. These outings became a valued tradition to group members. Transportation was provided for the girls through van service, volunteers and the workers themselves.

The group has always been co-led. The co-workers serve as a source of stimulation and support for each other as they consistently deal with the testing, acting-out and generally provocative behavior of the group members. There has been continuity of leadership with one of the present workers being with the group for the last four years, and with only one change of co-leader in that time.

The Group Members

The information about each member's background is being offered to illustrate the deprivations and hardships these children have endured and to heighten the understanding of the source and depth of their neediness.

Marsha is the oldest of four children in a single parent family where there has been chronic neglect and disorganization. At the age of nine, Marsha had to assume parental responsibilities for her siblings, including preparing them for school, fixing their meals, and disciplining their behavior. She was especially frustrated by her inability to do the latter. When referred, Marsha was a shy, immature, and pouty fifth grader who was habitually teased by her peers.

Barbara, the youngest of three in a single parent family, has experienced chronic neglect, social isolation, and lives with fear of unpredictable violent outbursts from her older brother. Her home has been condemned by the board of health, and she has not been taught basic personal hygiene practices. It is difficult to believe that she bathes and brushes her teeth once a week, as she claims to do, since her hair, body and clothes are always dirty. She has no friends outside of the group and is constantly ridiculed by her peers. She occasionally retaliates with a few angry words, but usually withdraws and truants from school.

Melissa, an attractive girl of at least average intelligence, is the next oldest of four girls in a single parent family. She and each of her sisters have been fathered by different men. At age seven, Melissa was sexually abused by her sister's father. Melissa testified against him in court and still fears that he will seek revenge against her. Melissa and her siblings have been both physically and verbally abused by their mother and have felt terrified and helpless when they observed their mother being battered by her boyfriends. Although on the surface, Melissa appeared to have good relationships with peers and adults, the provocative quality of interactions with others became apparent shortly after she joined the group.

Trudy is the oldest of three children of divorced parents. It has been especially difficult for Trudy, who is intellectually and emotionally handicapped, to deal with the instability brought upon by her parents' ineptness and eventual separation. She is often inappropriately dressed, unclean and physically tired because of having been moved from one to the other parent's apartment during her sleeping hours. Trudy is a shy, over-anxious girl who is the target of constant teasing from peers and has difficulty reacting without hostility to genuinely friendly overtures.

Kay, an only child of a two parent family, was sexually abused by her father for at least four years beginning when she was age six. Her father was prosecuted but returned home after a short prison sentence. Both parents are intellectually and socially limited, and her mother has had several "nervous breakdowns" for which she takes anti-psychotic medication. Kay's parents have difficulty setting appropriate limits on her behavior. Though Kay's school performance is passing, she is seen as belligerent and a troublemaker by school authorities.

Rosalie is the eldest of four siblings, all of whom have been in foster care for years and for whom adoption planning is currently underway. Rosalie's mother's own history of physical and sexual abuse did little to prepare her to fulfill her parental role. Rosalie experienced severe physical abuse and witnessed her mother's periodic suicidal attempts and beatings from boyfriends. Although intellectually, Rosalie is aware that her mother is incapable of providing for her, she has not given up the fantasy of returning home. She frequently runs from foster placements and acts out her rage through physical assaults on her mother during visits to her home.

Tina is the eldest of four children and lives with her mother and stepfather. Tina's father was killed in an explosion when she was eight years old. His tragic death resulted in her mother's severe depression and chronic neglect. Tina had to fend for herself as well as care for her younger siblings. Her anger and resentment of her situation was played out through teasing and assaulting her siblings.

The Group Experience Unfolds

During the ten week pilot project in 1979, the girls were on their best behavior. They sat politely, accommodated the groupworker's directions and expectations, discussed the issues the workers raised, played fairly, ate their snacks politely and helped clean up without hesitation.

This easy beginning lulled workers into a false expectation that groupwork with these girls would not be so difficult after all. If this had remained a short-term experience, the workers would have been left with a limited perspective of groupwork with this population, for the next year, the reality proved quite different. Meetings typically consisted of loud shouting, pillow fights, running out of the room to different parts of the building, either singly or en masse, bouncing on furniture and worst of all, picking on Trudy, who emerged as the group's scapegoat. To and from meetings, the girls would argue and throw food and each other's possessions out of the vehicle in which they were riding. This was a difficult time for the groupworkers, whose attempts to set limits on the angry and uncontrolled acting-out behavior usually met with failure.

This stage was also marked with intense rivalries between the developing subgroups. The self-proclaimed three musketeers emerged as leaders while the others worked hard to avoid verbal abuse from them. The three-Ms could be cooperative or provocative depending on their mood. The girls were all united, however, in their anger at the workers for not being able to set limits and protect them from their own anger and destructive behavior. Their ambivalence was demonstrated through each subgroup's attempt to elicit protective responses from the workers while claiming favoritism when the workers intervened accordingly.

Initially, the workers responded to their teasing of Trudy and sometimes Barbara with "Would you like it if someone behaved this way with you?" or "How do you think Trudy feels when you do this?" The three-Ms response would invariably be that if they did not want to be treated that way then they should not be so "stupid," act so "strange," or say or do the things they do. The workers often felt immobilized in the face of the apparent logic they presented.

The girls' anger, acting-out and scapegoating behavior became a primary concern of the groupworkers, who developed feelings of professional inadequacy and frustration at not being able to protect Trudy from the painful scapegoating she was receiving. It was at this point that they asked the agency to provide groupwork consultation.

Groupwork Consultation Begins

The Director of Social Work approached the groupwork consultant, told her the background of the group and suggested a consultation format of monthly meetings with the entire social work department (approximately ten to twelve people). This group consultation format was suggested in order to encourage other staff members to begin groups and also because many of the other social workers served as caseworkers to the families involved. In this way, more information would be available to all the professionals concerned.

At the first meeting with the staff, the consultant asked the co-leaders to identify their questions and concerns. They indicated that their biggest frustration was in not being able to do real "therapy" with the girls because so much time was spent in limit-setting and in activities. The consultant recognized this as a limited perspective of therapy which is carried out primarily through discussion and which does not require the limit-setting demanded by contagious acting-out behavior within the context of a group. She believed the first thing to do would be to provide a more appropriate frame of reference within which to study this experience and, therefore, recommended starting with a "mini course" on groupwork which would serve as a foundation for future discussion. The five sessions would include group development theory, limit-setting as a therapeutic intervention, and activities as a therapeutic tool.

Following these sessions, the plan was for the groups' co-workers to circulate process recordings and summaries of group meetings, along with issues they wished to discuss before each monthly consultation. However, when the time came, the workers did not follow through with this material and many sessions were spent "chatting" about the group in an unstructured, unfocused way that did not maximize the constructive use of consultation sessions. The consultant repeatedly asked for material that could serve as an organizing matrix for discussion and it was never forthcoming.

In a sense, the consultant was caught up in a potential power and control struggle with the staff and attributed their reluctance to bring in material to three specific reasons:

1. It was additional work for already overworked social workers.

2. It was written work and most social work practitioners are "doers" rather than "writers."
3. Most importantly, the workers were not feeling *good* about the work they were being asked to expose in detail to all of their colleagues.

Two particular incidents serve to illustrate this last point. One occurred in early February when one of the co-leaders thought it was time to start discussing the termination process for the group which was not scheduled to end until mid-June. Her eagerness to end the experience was obvious. A more direct indication occurred when the other co-leader remarked, "I feel terrible about how angry I get when the girls act so badly."

The consultant clarified and acknowledged the normalcy of their feelings and made the following responses:

1. The acting-out they faced was not a reflection of worker failure. The problems the workers were encountering were the very reasons they had started the group. They could not expect that the impulsive and angry behaviors that took nine years of full-time living to develop could be reversed in only months of one and one half hour weekly meetings. It was to be expected that the girls would not initially respond with reasonable behavior to each other or to the workers; that they would need an unusually long testing period before they could develop feelings of trust.
2. In spite of feeling inadequate, there were many things the workers were doing right. Their consistent giving to and caring about the group members in and of itself was helpful to these girls who had never before experienced adults in this way. The workers were building a foundation for the future, even though the only evidence of success so far was each girls' steady attendance and participation. The workers needed reminding that something important must have been happening to keep the girls as engaged in the group as they were.
3. The workers needed to relieve themselves of the guilt induced by thinking of their anger as a compromise of their own professionalism. Their feelings were normal responses, on the conscious and unconscious level, to the reality of the girls' provocative behavior which the workers understandably felt as consistent assaults on their total beings. To be sure, the work-

ers did not have the luxury of acting-out their anger and indeed, they did not. Their feeling angry, however, did not warrant the guilt they were experiencing.

The other workers joined in support of their colleagues and confessed to feeling grateful that the group was not their assignment. They often observed the girls running through the agency hallways on meeting days and knew how uncontrollable they were. They added their feelings of admiration for the workers apparent resiliency in the face of such difficult work.

Through the combination of the positive reinforcement for their efforts and skill, the support from their colleagues and the new perspective of the work they were doing, the workers began to look forward to consultation as an opportunity for help and began providing written material. The study process of the group could then begin in earnest.

Major Points in Consultation During the Early Group Phase

The issues addressed at this point apply not only to groupwork with abused youngsters, but also to practice with most acting out young people. Although the points raised here are not new, there is value in applying them specifically to work with this population.

The Therapeutic Value of Activities

The consultant reinforced the concept of program as a therapeutic tool by focusing on instances in which the normal day to day activities carried out at group meetings could be used as part of the therapeutic process. For example, the workers had established a tradition of celebrating each member's birthday with a cake and candles. During the consultation, the social workers explored the opportunities for therapeutic intervention that the birthday parties provided. They recognized that an intervention as simple as directing discussion towards the way birthdays were celebrated at home could lead to revelations of disappointments and feelings of being deprived of normal, happy childhood experiences. This discussion would be tolerable to the girls' within the context of an experience offering compensation for the deficits they identified.

The social workers also reviewed the value of activities as a vehicle for creative expression and the promotion of a sense of mastery.

These girls were all low achievers who had few other opportunities to develop and take pride in their creative abilities.

The value of art and drama as a stimulant and channel for the expression of personal material was also explored. Delson and Clark have written about their success with these activities in their groupwork with a similar population.[4] It was also recognized that activities provided structures to facilitate group interaction. The member interdependence created by group projects went far to foster cooperation, camaraderie and shared satisfaction from group achievement.

The Recognition and Acceptance of Members' Angry Feelings

There was much discussion about the importance of recognizing, addressing and accepting the angry feelings the girls repeatedly expressed through verbal tirades and acting-out behavior. In their frustration, the workers had taken a common sense approach of asking the provocateurs, "How would you feel if that was done to you?" This had proven to be an ineffective intervention. In its place, it was suggested that the workers communicate their recognition and acceptance of the anger behind the acting-out behavior. Simply remarking "you sure seem angry" would be much more helpful than apparent chastisement directed at the behavior alone. The discussion could then be led to the exploration and identification of the other factors in their lives that keep their anger so close to the surface and result in their over-reactions to each other.

This acceptance of anger is critical to work with victims of any injustice. It is important to convey to such populations that the therapeutic situation (in this case, the group) is not a "let's pretend" land where people are expected to only have "nice" feelings. The workers needed to take advantage of every opportunity if they were to help the girls be in touch with and subsequently constructively deal with the terrible anger they deserved to feel. At times the workers served as role models for the appropriate expression of anger by communicating their own frustration when they felt provoked by the girls. The workers' expression of their own anger without any retaliatory behavior towards the offenders helped the group reach its normative crisis; e.g., the point at which the members realized that the norms in the group were different than in the other places in their lives.[5] These adults would not turn against them as others had done. This dynamic is a major aspect of the power and control stage of group development and is a powerful component of the therapeutic process.

Developing Ground Rules for Group Behavior

It was critical for the workers to make the distinction between accepting angry feelings while not accepting destructive behavior. The workers were urged to introduce and repeat the idea over and over that anger and destructive behavior do not have to go together; e.g., "I know you are angry but I can't let you destroy the furniture. We will have to end the meeting early if you don't stop." It was recommended that during the group's calmer moments (perhaps at refreshment time), the girls be directed to discussions of what they thought they should try to do when they felt themselves losing control, and what seemed reasonable for the workers to do to help them gain it back. The girls did, in fact, engage with the workers in establishing a working agreement for these difficult times. To be sure, the acting-out behavior continued for months in spite of these lapses into reasonable discussions and the workers doubted they were making any progress.

Consistent Non-Retaliatory Worker Response

Although many meetings ended disastrously from the workers' perspective, i.e., with wild, uncontrolled behavior, the fact of their beginning the next meeting with a show of eagerness to see the girls again conveyed a message of "we accept you as you are." One social worker said this concept reminded her of the Jewish Sabbath which considers each Friday night a new beginning; a clean slate. It was imperative that the workers consistently maintain this approach if the destructive cycle of rejection of the girls set up everywhere else in their lives was to be broken.

The Group Experience Continues

Fortified by the support they received from the consultant and their colleagues, the workers were able to return each week with renewed energy and ability to withstand the "worker abuse" they were experiencing. Obvious results began to show in the group's third year. Though power and control issues were still prevalent, periodic meetings or parts of meetings began to emerge which suggested that the group was flirting with intimacy, identified by Garland et al. as the third stage of group development.[6]

At the start of this year, the girls poignantly revealed experiences of being victims of abuse and shared their feelings of anger and helplessness. Rosalie stood up to demonstrate how she was forced to stand in a corner while being beaten with a strap across the back of her legs. Melissa told how she was trapped in her room while her mother was being beaten by her boyfriend, only to have her attempts to telephone for help impeded by him. In a sense the girls were playing ''can you top this,'' but the quality of the discussion was intense and serious. As the girls listened to each other, they tried to offer advice, while registering their indignation of the unfairness of it all. The workers supported how justifiable their anger was and avoided the temptation of asking the girls to ''understand'' the source of their parents' behavior. While ultimately this could help the girls see their situations more objectively and work against their incorporation of feelings of guilt for uncommitted crimes, such discussion is more effective at a later point. At this point, it was important that the girls receive support for their feelings of anger at the injustices they repeatedly endured. By recognizing the true source of their feelings and encouraging verbal expression of their anger about it, the workers were helping to relieve the pressure which forced the girls to act out their feelings against surrogate villains. While the revelations of abuse were being made, the workers also directed discussion to ways of dealing with the incidents. The group suggested to Melissa that when she feared being assaulted, she should run to her room and scream out the window for help. Kay was told to make sure she was never left alone with her father.

The more the girls revealed of their situations, the more overwhelmed with helplessness the workers felt. The extent of the abuse was greater than anyone had known and the workers felt the emotional impact of knowing there was only so much that they or the girls could do about it. The workers were flooded with feelings of wanting to heal their wounds and spoke openly during consultation sessions about the frustrations they felt in this regard.

During this time, the girls began to make references to the workers as parental figures. They volunteered what they believed to be reasonable and effective ways to be disciplined and told the workers they were preparing them to be ''good mothers.'' This appears to have been their way of separating out the workers as the good parents from their own bad ones, while reinforcing the stance the workers had established with them. The workers silently hoped they, in turn, were doing the same, that is, preparing the girls to be ''good mothers.''

For several weeks at a time, the girls would use the group to openly discuss their situation and their feelings, only to engage again in acting-out and scapegoating behavior. However, during the apparent regressive stages, the girls seemed to attempt to maintain the workers continued acceptance of them by writing messages on the blackboard or creating greeting cards declaring "Joan and Karen are nice" or "we love you." The earlier "splitting" phenomenon in which the girls had separated out the "good workers" from the "bad parents" was now replaced by the workers symbolizing both the good and the bad.

As this phenomenon developed, the workers had to face and cope with the results of both the positive and negative transferences projected upon them. As the negative feelings towards their parents became accessible through expressions directed towards the workers, the girls were helped to recognize the true source of their anger. The workers validated the girls' statements about the unfairness of their situations and encouraged them to ventilate their anger at those who had hurt and exploited them. Rosalie stated with emotion that she sometimes hated her mother for her actions, and the other girls spoke similarly about their parents.

Therapists have recognized the therapeutic importance of re experiencing the pain and suffering that resulted from abusive events of the past rather than simply recalling the event without the accompanying feelings.[7] Based on this, Kindard indicates,

> The implication for treatment of abused children is clear: therapy must give the child an opportunity to recognize and explore feelings about being abused.[8]

In contrast to earlier phases of group development, those feelings were now accessible to the girls and the workers.

Another source of the girls' anger toward the workers may have resulted from realities in the present. They may well have shared the workers' frustration about the limitations of the help available to them. At times, the girls may have felt teased by their one and a half hours per week with women who showed them a more consistently satisfying pattern of adult-child relationships than others they had experienced, and which subsequently made their own realities harder to accept.

Thus, this phase of the group was fraught with a wide range of intrapsychic and interpersonal emotional dynamics. The girls felt affection and anger towards the workers and each other along with a fear of setting themselves up for rejection and guilt for their provocative behavior. They also felt relief at being able to express their rage about their situations and a growing sense of themselves as people apart from their families. The workers also felt both affection and anger toward the girls, sadness about what they were learning about their lives and guilt for not being able to do more for them. The consultation sessions provided a forum within which the workers could study and work on their own feelings and reactions in order to remain effective therapists.

During the latter part of this year, the girls began to express their interest in boys and their own emerging sexual feelings. Kay was the first to refer to sexual activity by proudly stating that she knew what a "B.J." was. This led to discussion about what, in fact, a "B.J." was, while Rosalie danced around the room using cotton to represent both men's and women's pubic hair, and giggling about photographs of "men's cheeks" she had seen. The workers took each of their comments seriously and answered some basic questions about the human body and sexual activity in a direct and open way, while recognizing and articulating how complicated feelings about sex and the body could be. Even though the workers expected the girls to have greater sophistication around sexual issues because of the experiences they had had, it was obvious that the girls, in some ways, were not different from other eleven and twelve year olds who handle confusion and discomfort with their new emotions and changing bodies through denial and distortions. Like other young adolescents, they were also in need of some basic information. In their work with a similar population, Knittle and Tuana shared this same observation. They wrote:

> The group is also a forum for teaching. The writers' experience has been that these young people have little knowledge and are grossly misinformed about human sexuality and birth planning.[9]

As the third year came to a close, one of the co-workers announced her pregnancy with her second child. This worker's example of responsible prenatal care served as an example of an alternative approach to mothering than what the girls had experienced themselves. In response to the girls curiosity about her situation, the pregnant worker shared considerations about family planning, her anticipations of sibling rivalry in her own household and how she was prepared to deal with it. The worker universalized these issues and encouraged the girls to explore sibling relationships in their own households.

Looking ahead to the next year of group, Melissa, a particularly sensitive young girl, enthusiastically predicted it was going to be exciting. She recognized how much work lay ahead for them all, and how ready they were to offer help and comfort to each other. The workers, too, were aware that the girls were ready for an openness and sharing that they had never before experienced.

Major Issues in Consultation During Middle Group Phase

By the third year of the group, the members had resolved many of the power and control issues and were moving into "intimacy," the Garland, Jones and Kolodny third stage of group development.[10] This stage was characterized in the group through evidence of familial transference (the workers were the "good mothers"), the revelation of personal material in a feeling way, the reduction (though not elimination) of acting-out behavior and mutual positive affect between the workers and the members. It was during this period that the same worker who earlier confessed her problem of angry feelings towards the girls now raised her feelings of "caring so much" for them.

As indicated earlier in this paper, the girls could not have been expected to reach this stage as readily as other youngsters because of their strong distrust of adults, poor peer relationships and problems with impulse control. It was the workers' handling of the earlier testing behavior and their open direct and gentle way of responding to the sexual material that fostered group movement in this direction. The consultant and other social workers were aware of their own discomfort in discussing the sexual material as evidence in the jokes and laughter during consultation sessions. Yet, it was the ability of the group's co-workers to respond to the girls' questions and concerns with the right combination of objectivity, understanding and genuine concern that gave the girls permission and encouragement to reveal the personal and often painful material to them and to each other.

The following are the major issues to be considered during this phase:

1. Even though the workers had helped the group to progress to

the point where they could provide therapy according to their original definition; e.g. talking directly about the problems they hoped to resolve, it was still important to maintain the supports for them that had been established earlier when they had felt more personal stress. Even though there were often times when there was no "advice" as such to be offered because of how skilled the workers were, the joint study process continued to be of great value to them and validated the job they were doing.

2. Three major sets of dynamics came together at this stage that needed to be recognized:

   a. In his discussion of the curative factors of group treatment, Yalom lists the opportunity within group situations for "family re-enactment."[11] It is during the intimacy stage of group development that this opportunity is especially strong. During this "family experience", however, the workers as parent figures played a more consistently positive role than was true in the girls' natural families. The repeated references to the workers as "mothers" indicated that the members were ready to accept the nurturing and caring the workers offered in spite of the negative meaning that "mother" also connoted. The workers had moved from being viewed as "authority figures" to "parent figures", and even with their human imperfections, could now begin to fill some, even if not all, of the terrible void left from the girls' painful pasts.

   b. Group development theory also indicates that identification with the workers is especially strong during this stage. The girls were now especially ready to be influenced by what the workers represented as people. The co-worker's pregnancy was particularly timely, for it exposed the girls to another view of parenting, one of love and concern for a child yet to be born. The girls had already learned that the workers would accept them. Now they, in turn, were ready to accept and incorporate what the workers represented. The workers were now role models of an alternative perspective of what parenthood and human relationships could be. They provided the girls with a new alternative of what they themselves could become.

   c. The girls were in early adolescence and according to Erickson, were searching for "identity vs. role confusion."[12] In a sense, the workers needed to support aspects of their role confusion and disequilibrium in order to help them discard the view of themselves as unworthwhile youngsters on the path to becoming abusing parents themselves. For these youngsters, it was important that the workers support the normal adolescent questioning of and rebellion against parental values and to reinforce their beliefs that they could develop into different kinds of adults with different life-styles. These individual and group development stages combined to make this stage very powerful.

3. The relationship between behavior and moral development must also be examined. In her study of children's concept of justice, Durkin[13] discusses Piaget's three periods in the development of the sense of justice. During the first period up until the age of seven or eight, justice is sought in the authority person. In the second period from about eight to eleven years old, it is found in reciprocity or the recognition that rules can be developed through mutual consent. By eleven and twelve years, justice continues to be sought in reciprocity, but there also emerges a consideration of "equity" or concern for the particular circumstances of the situation being judged

Translating this to the view of the world as seen through the eyes of an abused child, it can be assumed that in his/her early years, the young child accepts his/her own "badness" because justice and morality is defined through the *maker* of the law (the parent). In early latency, it is defined through the *letter* of the law. This dynamic could also serve to reinforce a low self-image because the child may have indeed been "bad" and broken a household rule. The ability to recognize that there are laws and moral codes that transcend parental reign entirely does not fully develop until early adolescence, the age that these girls had reached.

It is at this point that the workers could help foster the girls' growing commitment to justice over obedience, to the *spirit* of the law. The workers supported the part of them that was ready to believe their treatment by parents were unfair, unwarranted and unjust. The greatest problems in the adult years of abused children develop from, among other dynamics, an incorporation of the belief in their own unworthiness. The workers attempted to help the girls believe that, through no fault of their own, they had been cheated of the nurturing parents they deserved to have. Only then could they begin to grieve this loss, put it aside, and work to develop constructive behaviors that would help them lead satisfying lives.[14]

The Group Moves into Its Fourth Year

As the fourth year of the group began, the revelations of abuse continued. Kay volunteered, ''my parents think I know too much about sex.'' With reaffirmation of group confidentiality, she revealed how she was sexually exploited and abused by her father from age five through nine. Melissa then told of how her sister's father sexually abused her and of her subsequent embarrassment and fear in having to testify in court at age seven. Rosalie spoke of how she was ''almost raped'' and of how her mother was raped. Thus the interwoven themes of sex and violence continued to unfold. The girls used the intimacy of the group to get in touch with the sadness of their lost innocence which underlay the anger expressed during the earlier stages of the group.

With increased openness, the girls attempted to deal with their complicated feelings concerning their incestuous and violent experiences while struggling with their normal adolescent issues. They showed great interest in the co-worker's advancing stages of pregnancy, while discussing the peer pressures they felt to use drugs and be sexually active with boyfriends.

In attempts to help the girls unravel the distortions caused by their earlier experiences, interventions focused on helping them examine the consequences of their behavior, gain greater self-awareness and achieve a sense of mastery and control over their own lives. The workers continually reinforced that the girls did have the power to exercise choice in the determination of their own futures. Melissa's independent decision to quit her modeling job because of the revealing clothes she was asked to model, and Rosalie and Marsha's saying ''no'' to boys who asked them to have sexual intercourse were greatly supported, with acknowledgement of how difficult and complicated such decisions were to make. Marsha brought in a questionnaire used by boys to rate the sexual experience and potential of girls. As the girls boisterously took turns answering the questions, the workers helped the girls reflect on how such self-disclosure would be used and asked to consider how this fit in with the goals they had established for themselves. The girls responded to the workers' questions with a growing ability for self-reflection.

Now when the girls would begin with their provocative, acting-out behavior and the workers offered feedback about its effect on others (including themselves), the girls could recognize that they frequently set themselves up for rejection. The group, in this way, became a laboratory for life in the social environment.

The positive feelings between the members continued to grow. Instead of teasing and picking on Trudy, the girls declared, "we like Trudy this year." When Kay noticed Trudy being teased at school, she asked her about it in group. All of the girls acknowledged how they too were teased by peers and tried to help Trudy deal with it. When Rosalie, who was dealing with many disruptions and uncertainties in her life, continued to act out of control, her behavior was no longer contagious. As she carried on, the girls recognized her behavior as a symptom of her distress and expressed their concern for her. The same piece of behavior which was typical at an earlier stage had different meaning now that the other group members had moved to a higher level of functioning. Rosalie subsequently engaged in suicide gestures, resulting in hospitalization. The group as well as the workers openly questioned what they might have done differently to have prevented this unfortunate episode. The workers helped the girls accept that they had done all they could under the circumstances they shared and that Rosalie was unable to respond more fully to what they offered. The workers also helped the girls identify the strengths they had that could keep them from doing the same.

Marsha too seemed to fall behind at the intimacy stage as reflected in her frequent absences. At one of the meetings, in the presence of the others, the workers opened with a discussion about the fear of closeness and asked Marsha directly if this could be an issue for her. This struck a responsive note in Marsha and, to the surprise of all the professionals involved, her attendance became much more regular thereafter.

During the pregnant worker's maternity leave from February through May, there was again an apparent regression to the earlier testing behavior. This time, however, the remaining worker also had to bear the brunt of the displaced anger for the worker who had "deserted" the group. This was a particularly difficult time for her, for, without the support of her co-worker's presence and with the group's existence threatened by the agency's financial problems, her energy and tolerance were at a low point. With continuing support from the groupwork consultant and colleagues and with the support offered by the girls themselves in response to her revelations of uneasiness with their acting-out behavior, the group survived this critical period.

This past year, the fifth in the life of the group, the issues have remained the same but discussion continues with growing openness and from new perspectives. The girls continue to discuss whether or not to have sexual intercourse and examine what boys' motivations are in wanting sex with them. They show off their hickeys and dispel myths such as French kissing causing pregnancy. They try to sort out the difference between love and infatuation. They recognize that they want their lives to be different from the lives of their parents and explore when in their lives they want to have children, under what circumstances and how to prevent unwanted pregnancy. As the family violence recurs, the girls are taking positive steps in dealing with it and have influenced their families to reach out for help as well.

Although there is evidence of increased self-awareness, there is also still reluctance to give up or alter certain behaviors. While Kay, Melissa and Marsha engage in sexually provocative behavior, Barbara fails to bathe, wash her hair, brush her teeth or wear clean clothes. Kay, whose aggressive behavior was tolerated in junior high, is now being suspended in high school.

In spite of this, the girls have offered genuine support to one another. Melissa, who once would not sit next to Barbara because of her poor personal hygiene, engaged in restyling Barbara's greasy hair and applying make-up to her dirty, oily face. At school, Melissa has come to Barbara's defense when made fun of by peers, claiming the injustice of judging others by appearance. When Melissa was in conflict with her mother and came to group with bruises running up and down her arm, Barbara invited her to come stay with her for respite. When Kay expressed embarrassment over beginning to menstruate, the girls gave helpful hints on clothes she could wear so that others would not know.

During the latter part of the year, group attendance became more and more irregular, so that on one occasion only one member showed up. In assessing the situation, it was speculated that perhaps the group had reached its potential as a vehicle for mutual help. The workers accepted this and suggested monthly meetings, while offering individual sessions in between for those who wished. After one month's break, the girls returned sharing many of the stresses they experienced in the elapsed time and adamantly requested a return to weekly meetings. The workers agreed since it was most apparent how stressful the lives of the girls continued to be and how essential the group's availability was in helping them cope.

What was known about the girls in the beginning of the group experience continues to be painfully true. They remain out of the social mainstream in their schools and neighborhoods and are still members of dysfunctional families. What was not known at the start was the extent to which they have suffered.

The story of their lives and of their group continues. No one knows how it will end nor the extent of the impact of the group on their development and on their futures. What is known is that the group has exposed the girls to relationships with adults and peers unlike any others in their lives. The group workers offered them unconditional acceptance as contrasted to the judgmental and punitive reactions of other adult authority figures such as parents, police and teachers. They have learned to form friendships, to understand them, and to value them. They have learned to reach out for support when in distress and to be supportive to others. They have acquired the capacity for self-reflection and the recognition of their ability to make constructive choices. These gains cannot guarantee a satisfying future, but surely increase their chances for happiness in a life that was set up for them to be an uphill struggle.

NOTES

1. E. Milling Kinard, "Mental Health Needs of Abused Children," *Child Welfare*, Vol. LIX, 8, Sept/Oct 1980, p. 451.

2. Beverely J. Knittle and Susan J. Tuana, "Group Therapy As Primary Treatment for Adolescent Victims of Intrafamilial Sexual Abuse," *Clinical Social Work Journal*, Vol. 8, 4, 1980, pp. 236-242.

3. Joan Thrower Tinn, "Group Care of Children and the Development of Moral Judgement," *Child Welfare*, Vol. LIX, 6, June 1980, p. 333.

4. Niki Delson and Margaret Clark, "Group Therapy with Sexually Molested Children," *Child Welfare*, Vol. LX, 3, March 1981, pp. 175-182.

5. James A. Garland, Hubert E. Jones and Ralph L. Kolodny, "A Model for Stages of Development in Social Work Groups," in *Exploration in Group Work*, edited by Saul Bernstein, Charles River Books, Boston, 1973, pp. 17-71.

6. Ibid.

7. See for example, S. Fraiberg, E. Adelson and V. Shapiro, "Ghosts in the Nursery: A Psychoanalytic Approach to the Problems of Impaired Infant-Mother Relationships," *Journal of the American Academy of Child Psychiatry*, Vol XIV, Summer 1975, pp. 387-421.

8. Kinard, op. cit., p. 461.

9. Knittle and Tuana, op. cit., p. 240.

10. Garland et al., op. cit.

11. Irvin D. Yalom, *The Theory and Practice of Group Psychotherapy*, Basic Books, Inc., New York, 1975.

12. Erik H. Erickson, *Childhood and Society,* W.W. Norton & Co., Inc., New York, 1963.

13. Dolores Durkin, ''Children's Concept of Justice: A Further Comparison with the Piaget Data,'' in *The Adolescent: A Book of Readings,* edited by Jerome M. Seidman, Holt, Rinehart & Winston, Inc., New York, 1960, pp. 559-567.

14. For a discussion of this concept applied to group work with abusive mothers, see Nancy C. Avery & Julianne Wayne, ''Group Development & Grief Therapy,'' *Social Work with Groups,* Vol. 1, 3, Fall 1978, pp. 289-298.

BOOK REVIEWS

THE PSYCHOSOCIAL DEVELOPMENT OF MINORITY GROUP CHILDREN. Gloria Johnson Powell, Senior Editor. *New York: Brunner/Mazel Publishers, 1983, 600 pp.*

The influence of race and ethnicity upon psychosocial development of children cannot be dismissed in the assessment of health and illness. However, it is widely acknowledged that curricula in professional schools are deficient in addressing the needs of children of color; material on this topic is very often relegated to just one class session, such as "the role of culture in assessment." The professional literature is also fraught with gaps in theory and research, making a systematic approach to understanding the psychosocial development of children of color virtually impossible.

The book edited by Gloria Johnson Powell represents a scholarly effort to present a comprehensive picture of the psychosocial development of children of color. According to Powell, "It is hoped that a textbook devoted to the psychosocial development of minority group children will make apparent the gaps in knowledge and research and encourage others to fill in the missing pieces. It is hoped that this first textbook in child psychiatry devoted to the social and emotional needs of minority group children will serve as an impetus to require all training programs in child psychiatry, social work, and psychology to include this area as one of the requirements in their curriculum" (p. 6).

This book consists of thirty-two chapters organized into six conceptual categories: "The Health Status of Minority Group Children"; "Psychosocial Development"; "Family Life Patterns"; "Mental Health Issues for Minority Group Children"; "Educational Issues Regarding Minority Group Children"; and "Research and

Social Policy Issues.'' It focuses on the following racial/ethnic groups in the United States: Alaskan Natives, American Indians, Blacks, Chinese, Filipinos, Japanese, Koreans, Pacific Islanders, and Puerto Ricans.

Powell's book is a welcome contribution to the field of mental health research and practice and, within a short period of time, will serve as a benchmark for future endeavors in the field. Its strengths lie in five key areas: (1) exceptional organization of content; (2) high quality of writing in most chapters; (3) diversity of groups covered; (4) multi-disciplinary approach to the subject; and (5) practice implications are feasible suggestions for implementation. Additionally, the chapters on Vietnamese (Daniel D. Le), Korean (Keun H. Yu and Luke I.C. Kim), and Filipino-American children (Roland A. Santos) are exceptionally well written and address the needs of the groups frequently ignored in the professional literature.

However, the book is not without limitations. One that has been identified by Powell is that not every racial/ethnic group is covered in all six of the conceptual categories of the book. Also, like most books with numerous authors, not all of the chapters are equally well organized and written or make new contributions to the field. Nevertheless, despite the above limitations, this is still an outstanding book.

Melvin Delgado
Associate Professor
Boston University School of Social Work
Boston

USE OF GROUPS IN SCHOOLS: A PRACTICAL MANUAL FOR EVERYONE WHO WORKS IN ELEMENTARY AND SECONDARY SCHOOLS. Joy Johnson. *Washington, D.C.: University Press of America, 1979, 133 pages.*

This book advances the theme that an individual's school life is seriously affected, one way or another, by groups in the system. It seeks to provide basic concepts about group development and functioning as well as practical interventions which can be used by ''everyone'' (group member, leader, teacher, principal, committee chairman, PTA president, social worker, parent, or counselor) in leading or administering groups. Short chapters are devoted to classroom groups at various ages, groups for "special" children, groups to help children cope, faculty and community groups.

Although entitled a "manual," this book appears primarily a personal account of the author's considerable experience as teacher/consultant/social worker. It includes bits of information, advice, examples, and paragraphs of questions to "step back and think about." The author advocates a "no-fault school" which starts with the assumption that "everyone is entitled to a good day" and is based on a supportive, rather than a blaming attitude.

The chapters on group theory and dynamics seem drawn from the author's experience. She describes, for example, (only) four basic maintenance roles that are needed in a group: (1) leader, (2) nurturer, (3) enabler, and (4) subject changer. Scapegoat, monopolist, and isolate are "negative roles." Further, she delineates four qualities essential for group participation: (1) safety, (2) something for you, (3) something to contribute, and (4) someone cares. There appears to be little reference to the wealth of literature on small group research or social group work concepts and practice. Discussion of group theory, development, and intervention seems, at best, incomplete. References to "leader participating positively or negatively," changing a "malfunctioning group into a well functioning group," and "working on process issues" often is without theoretical grounding. Discussion of group stages is superficial and almost ignores termination, an area I suspect is frequently forgotten in schools. (Children suddenly find a group or class over and their teacher gone, without the essential process of review, evaluation and "letting go.") Discussion of goals and composition is useful, but there is no reference to establishing a contract. As in subsequent chapters on specific populations, the attempt to cover so many issues and to relate to everyone results in fractures. Alternative texts on basic groupwork and task groups would be advisable if professionals want to develop competency in leading or administering groups in the school setting.

This book would seem to have the greatest appeal to teachers, especially the examples of creative curriculum (e.g., involving a group of active boys in helping younger children how to read a calendar), aids in problem solving, and attention to faculty groups and committees. Of universal appeal is Chapter 5, which explains the correlation of child development and group readiness, as well as the importance of cooperative activities and group learning in grades

K-III. The book's greatest contribution seems its recognition and illustration of groups as basic and powerful in the school system. It provokes one to look beyond the individual or apparent content to group process and larger group issues. It makes an appeal for a supportive educational environment.

Trudy K. Duffy
Assistant Clinical Professor
Boston University School of Social Work
Boston

GROUP THERAPIES FOR CHILDREN AND YOUTH. Charles E. Schaefer, Lynnette Johnson, Jeffrey N. Wherry. *San Francisco, Washington, London: Jossey-Bass Publishers, 1982.*

The preface to *Group Therapies for Children and Youth* says that the goal of the book is to provide a practical and comprehensive handbook of the group therapies done with children aged four through adolescence. The authors state that the book covers the major theoretical approaches: psychoanalytic, behavioral, transactional analysis. Diagnostic groups are included in the section on theoretical orientations, because the authors believe they represent an innovative approach. The book consists of 126 fairly extensive abstracts of the content of articles from approximately 65 journals, followed by a commentary which at times contains the authors' judgments of the particular merits or lack thereof of the approaches described in the article. It also contains shorter summaries, "Additional Readings" after each section. A listing of the headings will give some idea of the scope of the book. Part I, "Therapeutic Approaches," contains the theoretical orientations, followed by "Types of Groups": play, activity, guidance, verbal interaction, psychodrama, arts and sports, parallel (parents and children). Part II is devoted to "Group Therapies for Specific Problems" which include articles on prevention for children at risk: developmental problems, the hospitalized and physically disabled, children of divorced parents, shy withdrawn children, and foster and adopted children. "Intervention Groups for Specific Problems": includes articles on groups concerned with peer relationships, anxiety and fear, autistic and psychotic behavior, mental retardation, learning disabilities and underachievement, school behavior problems, impulsive aggressive behavior, delinquency, and substance abuse. These articles are largely from the 1970s, 60s and a few in the 50s, 40s, even a classic of the 1930s, and several in 1980. The *International Journal of Group Psychotherapy* has the largest number of reviews. I may have missed the presentation of articles from *Social Work with Groups* which began publication in 1977. This may speak to this journal's publication of articles about children and youth or to its not coming up on the computer search of relevant journals. I was sorry to note how few articles came out of the social work group literature, although the Garland, Kolodny and Jones social group work model for stages of group development did comprise a section of the Introduction along with a mention of Konopka and Redl.

The author's method of presenting the descriptions of most of the articles is excellent. It is quite detailed and gives the reader the substance of the content, not just a cursory statement of the principles or techniques as many abstracts do. The reader who has a firm base in theory and practice can make his or her own judgement of the merits of the therapeutic assumptions and interventions which are presented. The authors provide some assistance with this by their comments on the articles, based on their own new version of what group therapy is supposed to be. This is covered to some extent in the 17 page introduction which discusses principles underlying group therapies, a brief history, some research, some group dynamics, stages of group development, and a list of references used as a base for this brief overview. This was not sufficient for me to understand the authors' remarks about some of the articles.

As a social work educator who teaches a course in therapeutic group work, I was once again struck in reviewing this book with the variety of approaches which are called group therapy and the variety of people who are concerned with group approaches to helping. I was made apprehensive when I thought about some of the assumptions about group treatment and the knowledge base underlying the assessment of the children's problems and the consequent treatment methods which are used by the journal authors. I knew I would never teach to my students some of the practice described. Then I became nervous that perhaps I was growing too conservative. I found reassurance in thinking about Slavson's article "When is a Therapy Group Not a Therapy Group?"

My basic question is how a collection of abstracts which is "eclectic in scope" can be useful to "clinicians in all disciplines." I may use the term "clinician" in a narrower sense than the authors. The articles reviewed represent very different levels of understanding, diagnostic acumen, different goals and techniques practiced by people with very different levels and kinds of education and practice in settings with very diverse functions. Perhaps the reader will look up articles from his or her favorite journals and be able to judge their merits from that professional perspective. My own professional perspective is that one should not use group interventions for which one is not educated. Part of education is to learn about the theory, practices and research of other disciplines, but I believe one needs a solid grounding to make judgements about what to use. This book does provide an opportunity to become acquainted with the ideas of a variety of writers and, unhappily, to discover how little research has been described which verifies or disputes prescriptions and claims about group treatment. Because there is no coherent framework of theory or practice, I do not see this book as a guide to practice to which someone would turn to find out how to work with a particular kind of group or work with a particular population. It is instead a reference book which gives excellent, well organized summaries of some of the group literature. It can be used by other authors and educators who wish to be more literate in their fields, find support for their own ideas, or be better teachers. Students and practitioners may also find it to be a good reference for information about the wide variety of group approaches currently in vogue.

Louise A. Frey
Professor of Social Work
Boston University School of Social Work
Boston

**The Advancement
of Social Work
with Groups**

*Seventh Annual Symposium
October 23–27, 1985
Hyatt Regency
New Brunswick, New Jersey*

ROOTS AND NEW FRONTIERS

A Call for Presentations (experiential workshops, papers, media presentations, and demonstrations) from practitioners, educators, administrators and researchers working with groups.

ISSUES & THEMES	SETTINGS
stage issues	settlement house
group process	YMCA, YWCA, JCCs,
member capacities	YMHA, YWHA
intervention strategies	camps
conflict	health
group purpose	schools
role of worker	child welfare
group activities	gerontology
support & self help	mental health
special populations	corrections
	substance abuse
	family & community agencies

Abstracts for presentations not to exceed two hours should be five hundred words long and include a statement about the main topic and basic premises. Where appropriate references should be made to empirical support for these premises. Please indicate (1) the target population to be addressed; (2) what type of audience participation is intended; (3) the particular audience to which your presentation is directed (e.g., new practitioners, educators, etc.).

A fifty word descriptive statement must accompany each submission, and workshops that offer participants the opportunity to experience different group modalities that benefit varying populations (e.g., disabled, ethnic, aged, etc.) are encouraged.

continued...

DEADLINE: January 30, 1985
NOTIFICATION OF ACCEPTANCE: March 15, 1985
SUBMIT TWO COPIES to:

Dr. Martin Birnbaum
Center for Social Work
Fairleigh Dickinson University
830–4 River Road
Teaneck, NJ 07666

FOR FURTHER INFORMATION contact:

Professor Marcos Leiderman
Rutgers University School of Social Work
George Street
New Brunswick, NJ 08903

The 7th Annual Symposium is sponsored by: The Advancement of Social Work with Groups, the journal of *Social Work with Groups,* The Haworth Press, Rutgers University School of Social Work, UMDNJ–Rutgers Medical School, UMDNJ–Community Mental Health Centers, and the faculties of the major schools of social work in the New Jersey, New York, Connecticut, Massachusetts and Pennsylvania areas in cooperation with major agencies.